As with many ancient Sa[...] of Nārāyaṇa beyond his [...]. He was evidently a devotee of the god Śiva, who is invoked in both the opening and concluding verses of the *Hitopadeśa*. Contemporary scholars suggest that Nārāyaṇa was a poet or a preceptor at the court of his patron Dhavala Ćandra, a prince or viceroy or provincial satrap of eastern India, who commissioned the work. This densely layered and textured masterpiece was composed between 800 and 950 AD. Nārāyaṇa was an erudite grammarian and philosopher as well as a consummate stylist with a full command of epigrammatic, lyrical, satiric and rhetorical modes. He interspersed his own stanzas with skilful selections and arrangements of extracts from traditional sources. These include the immortal *Pañćatantra*, the *Ramayana* and the *Mahabharata*, the *Puraṇas*, the *Manusmrti*, manuals on economics and statecraft inspired by Ćāṇakya's *Arthaśāstra*, and famous literary and dramatic compositions.

~

Aditya Narayan Dhairyasheel Haksar was born in Gwalior and educated at the Doon School and the universities of Allahabad and Oxford. He spent many years as a career diplomat, and went on to become India's High Commissioner to Kenya and the Seychelles, and later the Ambassador to Portugal and Yugoslavia.

He has translated various classics from the Sanskrit, including the stories of the *Pañćatantra*, the plays of Bhasa and Daṇḍin's *Daśa Kumāra Ćaritam*. The last two translations were published by Penguin as *The Shattered Thigh and Other Plays*, and *Tales of the Ten Princes*.

NĀRĀYAṆA

The Hitopadeśa

Translated from the Sanskrit
with an introduction by
A.N.D. Haksar

PENGUIN BOOKS

PENGUIN BOOKS

USA | Canada | UK | Ireland | Australia
New Zealand | India | South Africa | China

Penguin Books is part of the Penguin Random House group of companies
whose addresses can be found at global.penguinrandomhouse.com

Published by Penguin Random House India Pvt. Ltd
7th Floor, Infinity Tower C, DLF Cyber City,
Gurgaon 122 002, Haryana, India

Penguin
Random House
India

First published by Penguin Books 1998

12 11 10 9 8 7 6

ISBN 9780144000791

Typeset in Palatino by Digital Technologies and Printing Solutions, New Delhi
Printed at Repro Knowledgecast Limited,

www.penguin.co.in

P.M.S.

For my daughter
Sharada
with all my love

Key to the Pronunciation of Sanskrit Words

Vowels:

The line on top of a vowel indicates that it is long.

a	(short)	as the u in b*u*t
ā	(long)	as the a in f*a*r
i	(short)	as the i in s*i*t
ī	(long)	as the ee in sw*ee*t
u	(short)	as the u in p*u*t
ū		as the oo in c*oo*l
e		is always a long vowel like the a in m*a*te
ai		as the i in p*i*le
o		as the ow in *o*wl

Consonants:

k, b and p are the same as in English

kh is aspirated

g   as in *g*oat

gh is aspirated

ć   as in *ch*urch or *c*ello

ćh is aspirated as in *chh*ota

j   as in *j*ewel

jh is aspirated

ṭ and ḍ are hard when dotted below as in *t*alk and *d*ot

ṭṭ is the aspirated sound

ḍḍ is aspirated

ṇ when dotted is a dental; the tongue has to curl back to touch the palate.

ṅ   as in ki*n*g

t   undotted is a soft sound as in *th*ermal

th is aspirated

d   undotted is a soft sound—there is no corresponding English sound, the Russian 'da' is the closest.

dh is aspirated

ph and bh are aspirated

There are three sibilants in Sanskrit: s as in song, ṣ as in *sh*ove and a palatal ś which is in between, e.g. Śiva.

Contents

Introduction

> *This work, entitled Heetopades, affordeth elegance in Sanskreet idioms, in every part and variety of language, and inculcateth the doctrine of Prudence and Policy.*
>
> —from the translation of Charles Wilkins

*T*he *Hitopadeśa* is one of the best known and most widely translated works of Sanskrit literature. It is a collection of animal and human fables in prose, illustrated with numerous maxims and sayings in verse, both intended to impart instruction in worldly wisdom and the conduct of political affairs. Couched in simple and elegant language, it was also meant to provide a model for composition and rhetoric. These features made it a popular 'reader' for students of Sanskrit in India from ancient to recent times.[1]

The *Hitopadeśa's* appeal as a compendium of sage advice in an attractive story form extended its currency beyond the confines of the original language. At the beginning of this century, the Indologist Johannes Hertel noted[2] that its translations already existed in Bangla, Gujarati, Hindi, Kannada, Malayalam, Marathi, Newari, Oriya, Tamil, Telugu and Urdu. The United States Library of Congress lists additional contemporary translations of the *Hitopadeśa* into Burmese, Dutch, English, French, German, Greek, Khmer, Russian, Spanish and Thai. Translations in Malay, Persian and Sinhala have also been recorded.[3] The work has been described as one of the most often translated from Sanskrit into European languages.[4] This was doubtless also because it was among the first Sanskrit texts encountered and studied by Europeans after the establishment of British rule in India.

The *Hitopadeśa* was the second work to have been

translated directly from Sanskrit into English.[5] This took place as early as 1787. The first work so translated was the *Bhagavad Gita*, three years earlier. The translator in both cases was Charles Wilkins (1749-1836), a merchant employed by the East India Company in Bengal. Wilkins also collaborated with the more celebrated scholar Sir William Jones (1746-94), who founded the Asiatic Society in Calcutta, and himself subsequently translated other Sanskrit classics. The first printed edition of the *Hitopadeśa* was published in Serampore along with some other Sanskrit texts in 1804 by Henry Colebrooke (1765-1837). It is appropriate here to pay tribute to these pioneers whose work first aroused modern interest in Sanskrit and helped to lay the foundation of Indological studies.

The Date, the Author, and the Locale

The *Hitopadeśa* contains quotations from the political treatise *Nītisāra* of Kāmandaki, and the play *Veṇīsamhāra* of Bhattanārāyaṇa, which date back to the eighth century AD. The earliest *Hitopadeśa* manuscript, found in Nepal, bears a date corresponding to 1373 AD. Between these two outer limits present scholarly opinion places its composition in the period 800 to 950 AD, or just over a thousand years ago.[6]

For almost a hundred years after its first rendition into English, contemporary scholars considered the author of the *Hitopadeśa* to be Viṣṇu Śarma, who is also the principal character and narrator in the work. It was only when the Nepal manuscript was discovered and a new critical edition of the text[7] prepared, that its two concluding verses came to light. The first of these names the author as Nārāyaṇa. The second names his patron Dhavala Ćandra, who commissioned the book.

As with many ancient Sanskrit authors, little is known about Nārāyaṇa beyond his name. From the text of the *Hitopadeśa* it is obvious that he was a person of considerable erudition, perhaps a court poet or preceptor, and evidently a devotee of the great god Śiva, whom he invokes both in the opening and concluding verses. He addresses Dhavala Candra by the titles 'Śrimat' and 'Māndalika' which have been rendered in the present translation as 'illustrious prince', but could also signify a viceroy or provincial satrap. The territorial and other details regarding the life and rule of this dignitary have still to be discovered.

It has been conjectured that the *Hitopadeśa* was composed in eastern India. Its manuscripts have been found in Nagari, Newari and Bengali scripts. One of the tales (I.viii) refers to tantrik rituals and sexual practices which were prevalent in that part of the country.[8] Two of its verse quotations from the *Rāmāyaṇa* (1.77 and 4.29) are available only in the Bengali recension of the epic.[9] Of the thirty-five geographical locations mentioned in the *Hitopadeśa* stories, at least nine can be placed definitely in eastern India, if Ayodhya and Varanasi are included in that region. By comparison, those which can be identified in the northern, western and peninsular regions are fewer. The totality of this data relevant to dating and location, taken together with the fact of the text's continued popularity in the east at the time of the British arrival, points to its origin during the last phase of the Pala empire, which dominated eastern India at the turn of the millennium.

The Nature of the Work

The nature of the *Hitopadeśa* is clearly defined in its prologue. The second verse names the work and asserts that its study gives knowledge of '*nīti*', apart from proficiency in language. Subsequent verses extol the merits of learning and knowledge. The work is a manual of *nīti*. This Sanskrit word, derived from a root which means to lead or to guide, carries the connotations of worldly wisdom, prudence and propriety, as well as appropriate policy and conduct or, by extension, politics and statesmanship. A portion of Sanskrit literature is entirely devoted to the subject of *nīti*. The *Hitopadeśa* expounds it in a popular form through fables and gnomic stanzas.

The work has also been placed in the Sanskrit literary genre of the *nidarśana kathā* or *exemplum*, a story which aims to teach by examples and is often satirical. The pattern is the familiar one of a frame tale emboxing others in turn. The basic narrative describes a king, worried that his sons lack learning and are becoming wayward. He summons an assembly of wise men and asks who among them can cause his sons to be 'born again' by teaching them *nīti*. The challenge is accepted by a great pandit named Viṣṇu Śarma, whose expertise in *nīti* parallels that of Bṛhaspati, the guru of all the gods. The princes are entrusted to Viṣṇu Śarma, and he instructs them by narrating the four books of the *Hitopadeśa*, each with its own mix of stories within stories illustrated with epigrammatic verses.

Relationship with the Pañcatantra

The structure of the *Hitopadeśa* is remarkably similar to that more ancient collection of tales, the *Pañcatantra*. Both works have an almost identical frame story, and the principal narrator has the same name. Their relationship has been described variously by modern scholars. Basham considered the *Hitopadeśa* to be a 'version' of the *Pañcatantra*, Keith a 'descendant', Winternitz a recast, while Dasgupta and De described it as 'practically an independent work'.[10] A detailed study made more recently by Ludwig Sternbach[11] demonstrated that the *Pañcatantra* provides the chief source of material for the *Hitopadeśa*. Nearly three quarters of the latter, including almost one third of its verses, were traced to the older work.

Nārāyaṇa has specifically acknowledged this source. In the ninth verse of his prologue, he names his four books and states that they have been composed by drawing from the *Pañcatantra* and another work. The version of the *Pañcatantra* from which he drew his material is, however, unknown at present. In some instances the *Hitopadeśa* text is nearer to the *Pañcatantra's* southern recension, in others to the Kashmiri, the Nepalese or even the old Syriac version.[12] Compared with the five books of the *Pañcatantra*, the *Hitopadeśa* has only four. In these the order of the older work's first two books—except as found in the Nepalese text—has been reversed; its third book has been divided into two; and parts of the fifth book have been incorporated into them. The fourth book of the *Pañcatantra* is mostly omitted in the *Hitopadeśa*, and at least ten of the latter's thirty-eight interpolated stories are not found in any *Pañcatantra* version at all. Of the over two hundred verses traced to various *Pañcatantra* versions, a majority are found in the first two books of the *Hitopadeśa*. Though mostly scattered, they also include some sequences such as 1.173 to 1.178 and 2.129 to 2.136 in the present translation.

Other Sources of the Hitopadeśa

Nārāyaṇa's 'another work' covers multiple sources. Sternbach's study categorizes them into three broad groups: *nīti*, *dharmaśāstra*, and other miscellaneous works. The first two are reflected mainly in the verse portions of the *Hitopadeśa*.

Apart from the *Pañcatantra*, Nārāyaṇa's single main source is the verse composition *Nītisāra* of Kāmandaki. Nearly ninety verses in the *Hitopadeśa* are quotations from this work. Devoted chiefly to the aspects of *nīti* that deal with political theory, most of these verses are contained in the third and fourth books. They discuss the subjects of diplomacy, war and peace. Good examples are verses 4.111 to 4.132, describing sixteen types of peace treaties, which are taken from the *Nītisāra*, 9.1 to 9.22. The majority of verses 3.69 to

3.84 are similarly derived.

The Nītisāra is based on a celebrated earlier dissertation on politics, the Arthaśāstra ascribed to Kautilya, also known as Cāṇakya. Nārāyaṇa mentions this legendary statesman (3.60) though, interestingly, he has no quotations from the Arthaśāstra. The Hitopadeśa does feature a large number of stanzas from various nīti verse anthologies named after Cāṇakya, such as the Vṛddha and the Laghu Cāṇakya, the Cāṇakya Sāra Samgraha and the Cāṇakya Rāja Nīti Śāstra. It also contains nīti verses from the Garuḍa Purāṇa and the well-known Nītiśataka of Bhartṛhari.

The term dharmaśāstra here refers to the vast body of literature dealing with legal and juridical precepts which acquired scriptural status in the course of time. Nārāyaṇa quotes about sixty verses from this category of works, his main sources being the Manu Smṛti and Books XII and XIII of the Mahābhārata. Others include the juridical works named after lawgivers like Gautama, Āpastamba and Baudhāyana.

The miscellaneous sources include the two epics, various Purāṇas, and well-known poetic and dramatic compositions such as the Śiśupālavadha of Māgha (3.96), the Kirātārjunīya of Bhāravi (4.103), and the Mṛcchakatika of Śūdraka (2.126). The verse numbers indicated within brackets are sample quotations in the Hitopadeśa from the last three works. Some of the Hitopadeśa material is also found in other collections of stories. For example, the tales of the woman with the two lovers (II.vi), and the faithful servant Vīravara (III.viii) also occur respectively in the popular collections, the Śukasaptati and the Vetāla Pañcaviṃśatikā. In the absence of a clearly established comparative chronology, who borrowed from whom is an open question. A number of Hitopadeśa verses are also found in the old Javanese and Pali literature of south-east Asia, and the Tibetan and Mongolian literature of Central Asia. In these cases too the primary sources are still to be determined.

The Hitopadeśa Verses

The over seven hundred verses interspersed in its prose text are a distinctive feature of the *Hitopadeśa*. Some of these, like the first two and the last three of the work, and the concluding stanzas of its first three books, are probably the author's own compositions. The others are direct or modified quotations. The book is thus as much a verse anthology as a compilation of fables on *nīti*.

Some of the verses selected by Nārāyaṇa occur in more than one work; some are still current in the form of proverbs and popular sayings. The famous verse 1.14, which is repeated as 4.134, is found in the *Garuḍa Purāṇa* (1.111), the southern (3.39) and the Nepali (3.32) *Pañcatantra*, the *Cāṇakya Nīti Darpaṇa* (12.14), as well as the *Vetāla Pañcaviṃśatikā*. Verse 1.71, which contains the often cited maxim 'Vasudhaiva Kutumbakam,' occurs in the *Pañcatantra* (5.38), the *Cāṇakya Nītiśāstra* (1.69) and, with a slight variation, in the *Vikramacaritam* (3.1).[13] Other well-known verses include 1.16, which is found, barring one word, in the *Bhagavad Gita* (17.20), and the now notorious 1.122, which is taken from the *Manu Smṛti* (9.3). The fine stanza 4.92 is from the Udyoga Parvan (40.21) of the *Mahabharata*,[14] and the satirical 4.105 from Bhartṛhari's *Nītisataka* (1.3).

Most *Hitopadeśa* verses are of the type known as *muktaka* or *subhāṣita*. This poetic form has been compared to the Persian rubai or the Japanese tanka.[15] A single stanza, the meaning or mood of which is complete in itself, it was composed in isolation or as part of a longer work. It dealt with a large variety of themes and, at its best, combined brevity with a felicitous condensation of thought. It was also often designed for easy memorization and quotation in an age when books were still few and handwritten. This mnemonic function led to a large number of such verses being composed essentially to convey information and advice on all kinds of subjects besides *nīti*, from medicine and mathematics to erotic techniques and military tactics.

The modern Sanskrit anthologist K.A.S. Iyer described[16] the *subhāṣita* as 'a pithy saying, embodying worldly wisdom, relating to one or more aspects of life, and often of a didactic character'. The *subhāṣita* on *nīti* may sometimes appear cynical but, in the words[17] of the late Harvard Sanskritist D.H.H. Ingalls, 'its purpose is neither to disparage the world, nor to flatter it, but to see it as it is. Accordingly, *nīti* verses dispense with elaborate ornaments; they are clipped, sententious, epigrammatic; and they include a wide range within their field of attention, for the real world contains good as well as bad'. These descriptions could well apply to the verses selected by Nārāyaṇa.

Nārāyaṇa as an Anthologist

The *Hitopadeśa* is no pale imitation or mere aggregation of its source materials. What gives it a refreshing identity of its own is the skilful way in which Nārāyaṇa selected and arranged his extracts from a wide range of other works, supplementing them occasionally with his own compositions and modifications to produce something distinctive. In the final stanza of the second book, he refers to his book as a garden or grove of pleasing stories. His art was essentially that of the compiler and the anthologist, assembling and presenting diverse tales and maxims in a manner which gave an additional cohesion and impact to the whole. His grouping of verses, in particular, is harmonious for the most part, and designed to emphasize the moral of each tale.

Nārāyaṇa also adds a sense of liveliness to many verses by having them recited by animal characters. The birds and the beasts of his tales comment on human foibles and discuss life's problems with solemn quotations from authoritative texts. This lends a tongue-in-cheek charm to some of the stories, such as that of the aged tiger (I.i) sanctimoniously citing the scriptures to lure a hesitant traveller close enough to be devoured; or the dog and the donkey (II.ii) discussing the responsibilities they bear to their master, the washerman, while he is in bed with his wife. By the time we arrive at the final frame story which encompasses the last two books, the animals are almost human. The war between the land birds and the water birds, with their vain and impetuous kings, wise and cautious ministers and time-serving courtiers, provides an opportunity for the animal characters to deliver stirring verse homilies on individual psychology and the rules of governance.

Text and Translation

Unlike the *Pañcatantra*, which exists in a number of recensions with notable differences, there is only one main version of the *Hitopadeśa*, though it may not be the ur-text. It has been critically edited several times, including by Max Müller in 1865. The longest text, containing 749 stanzas, is the 1864 edition of J. Johnson, while the shortest, which contains 655 stanzas and incorporates for the first time the Nepal manuscript already mentioned, is that of P. Peterson, published in 1887. A scholarly comparison of all the main editions concludes that 'the textual differences between the various editions of the *Hitopadeśa* are of little importance'.[18]

The text used for the present translation is M.R. Kale's edition, first published in 1896.[19] With 733 stanzas, it stands between the shortest and the longest texts, and is also the most recent of the main critical editions. One stanza (1.116) which is partly suppressed in Kale's text, doubtless on grounds of obscenity, has been taken for this translation from Peterson. Kale's numbering of the stories and the stanzas has been retained. They are referred to with roman and Arabic numerals respectively, the first digit indicating the book. In addition, each story has been given a subtitle for ready reading.

The *Hitopadeśa* has been translated into English several

times. Apart from Wilkins' pioneering version, another rendering by Sir Edwin Arnold appeared in 1861 with the title *The Book of Good Counsels*. The same title was used by B. Hale-Wortham in his 1906 translation. Other translations include some literal ones for students wishing to follow the original text, as well as edited versions for children.

The present translation attempts to render the Sanskrit text faithfully in a contemporary idiom which may also convey something of the particular flavour of the original. The last consideration would also explain the occasional use of archaisms, specially in translating the prose parts. The translation of the verses involved a further consideration. In most, any poetic or ornamental literary content is low or even absent. The emphasis is didactic, and the form is gnomic and often mnemonic. It was felt that these characteristics would best be reflected through a rendition in simple rhyming verse of the doggerel type. A prose translation could have given more scope for precision, but less for conveying the spirit of the original. The varying quality of the verse renderings corresponds to the variations in the originals. Some of them have a fine flourish while others are bald statements for example 4.140 and 4.141, the two concluding stanzas of the work; in other cases the moods differ, as with 3.69 to 3.76 on the subject of war, and 4.68 to 4.77 on the transitoriness of life. In a few instances, the verse translations include additional explanatory lines, which have been put in parentheses.

The Sanskrit mode for addressing a king, *deva*, which literally means god, has been rendered mostly as 'sire'. The honorific pronoun *bhavat*, has been translated variously as 'sir', 'Your Honour', or 'Your Majesty', depending on who is addressing whom. The word *nīti* has been rendered in one of its several meanings in accordance with the context. *Dharma*, another word with multiple connotations, has usually been translated as 'virtue' or 'righteousness'; occasionally it has been left in the original, in which form it has already entered the English language. Proper nouns have been retained in the original. In the case of animals, an English near-equivalent or derivative has also been added. A few names have been split into two words, for example 'Viṣṇu Śarma'. Diacritics have been discarded in the transliteration of some names still in common usage.

Like any good anthology, the *Hitopadeśa* can be savoured best by dipping into it from time to time, as compared to reading it from end to end. Opened at any page, it can reveal a fable or a stanza which may strike a responsive chord, provoke dissent or make a point to think about. At the same time its stories have a pattern which rewards sequential reading. The present translation also endeavours to retain these qualities which have contributed to the original text's popularity over the centuries.

~

I still possess a dog-eared copy of 'Mitralābha', the first book of the *Hitopadeśa*, which I read as a student many years ago. In preparing the present translation I have profitably consulted Kale's Sanskrit commentary and the notes appended to his edition of the text. I am grateful to David Davidar, Chief Executive Officer and Publisher of Penguin Books (India), for asking me to undertake this translation, and giving me extended time for completing it. I would like to thank Smriti Vohra for editing the typescript. Parts of my translation were earlier read by Madhav Dar, to whom I am indebted for various comments. Thanks are also due to J. Padma Rao of the Indian Embassy in Washington DC, and V.K. Jain, Director, Ministry of External Affairs Library, New Delhi, for helping with the reference material; and to my children Sharada and Vikram Haksar for obtaining information from the US Library of Congress. I am obliged to Dr Bibekananda Banerjee of the Asiatic Society, Calcutta for details of the Newari manuscript shown on the cover of this book. Most of all I wish to thank my wife Priti for her patient, critical and always helpful scrutiny of the drafts, and for her unfailing encouragement and support at every stage of their preparation.

December 1997   A. N. D. H.
New Delhi

Prastāvikā

Prologue

$\mathcal{M}$ay success tend good people's labour (1)
By grace of him, on whose brow gleams
The moon's delightful crescent favour,
Bright as foam on Gangā's streams.

Study of these counsels benefic, (2)
Gives to speech felicity,
Skill in words, diverse and specific,
And knowledge of right policy.

The wise will strive for wealth and learning, (3)
As if to time and age immune;
But not delay good works, discerning
That death may strike one very soon.

Of all things, learning, seers declare (4)
It best by far, beyond compare:
Always prized, it can't decay,
Nor be seized or forced away.

Learning even gives the lowly (5)
Access to high company,
And thence to fortune: flowing slowly,
Streamlets too may join the sea.

Learning teaches manners gentle, (6)
And they bring gainful patronage;
The latter leads to wealth, essential
For bliss and virtue in this age.

Learnings twain, of sword and science—   (7)
From both can glory be expected;
But one, with age, invites alliance
With ridicule; the other always is respected.

May minds still young be fired here   (8)
By knowledge set in guise of fable,
As fresh clay pots are moulded, ere
Their baking into vessels stable.

Gaining Friends and Splitting Partners,   (9)
Making War to Peace attain:
Drawing on the *Pañcatantra*
And other works, we here explain.

On the banks of the river Bhāgīrathī there lies a city called Pāṭaliputra. In it there reigned a king named Sudarśana, who was possessed of all the royal virtues. Once this monarch heard someone recite two verses:

'It explains even things supernal,   (10)
It sees through every doubt with speed.
Science is the eye eternal—
Who knows it not is blind indeed.

Youth, great wealth, authority,   (11)
And lack of discrimination:
Each one can cause calamity—
More so, their aggregation.'

The king was already upset as his sons had learnt nothing, become wayward, and never followed the scriptures. Hearing these verses, he began to worry:

'What is the point of having a son   (12)

With neither wit nor piety?
Like the eyes of a sightless one—
For nothing good but agony.

Better than a foolish son,   (13)
Is one deceased or never born.
The pain he gives at least is brief;
The former causes lasting grief.

'Moreover,

With constant rounds to life decreed,   (14)
Both birth and death are no surprises,
But truly born is he indeed,
By whose birth his family rises.

They are not marked, not even once,   (15)
When one counts merit in this life:
The mother of such worthless sons
Had better been a barren wife.

In penance, valour, charity,   (16)
Whose repute is not evident,
In learning nor in earning, he
Is but his mother's excrement.

'Furthermore,

Better than a foolish brood   (17)
Is a single child with merit.
Darkness doth one moon preclude:
A thousand stars can't do it.

Penance hard in holy places   (18)
Is needed if you want but one
Child with wit and all the graces,

A wealthy and obedient son.

Steady income, perfect health,   (19)
A loving and sweet-tempered wife,
Sons obedient, learning's wealth:
O King, these make a happy life.

Will many sons a blessing be   (20)
To add up in the numbers' game?
Just one who helps the family,
Is better for the father's name.

The wanton mother is an enemy,   (21)
The debtor father is a foe.
An enemy is the wife too pretty;
The unread son is no less so.

Maidens are no better than   (22)
Poison for the aged man;
And the public assembly
For the man in penury;
As eating is for any person
Who is suffering indigestion;
And learning for the person who
Puts it not to practice true.

Lauded is the person dextrous   (23)
No matter what his pedigree.
Though of purest cane, a stringless
Bow will always useless be.

Alas, my sons, you ignored learning;   (24)
Your nights were spent in luxury.
As oxen muddy waters churning
Among the cultured you shall be.

'But how can I get my sons educated now? For,

> With beasts we share a similar nature (25)
> In fear and hunger, sex and rest.
> Virtue is man's special feature:
> Without it, he's a beast at best.

> Virtue, wealth, salvation, pleasure: (26)
> The life where these aims absent be—
> A he-goat's udder gives the measure
> Of its sheer futility.

'But it is said,

> Actions, wealth, and life's duration, (27)
> Learning, and the way one dies:
> Fate makes of these determination
> While in one's mother's womb one lies.

'And, further,

> Gods too bow to destiny, (28)
> For fate no exceptions makes.
> Śiva goes naked, as we see,
> And Viṣṇu sleeps on beds of snakes.

'What is more,

> "What will not, will never be, (29)
> What will, must come to pass for sure."
> For every care this remedy,
> Why not drink and fret no more?

'But these are the idle words of those who have no capacity to do anything.

Though fortune may be in your favour,   (30)
Effort you should not disdain.
Oil from seeds of sesamum never
Without pressing will you gain.

'And,

Cowards say that "destiny gives",   (31)
But fortune comes to him who strives.
Shun fate, and do the manly deed—
No harm if efforts don't succeed.

As one wheel moves the chariot never,   (32)
So luck won't work without endeavour.

'And, further,

What men call fate is only fruit   (33)
Of actions in their previous birth.
So, from your habits sloth uproot,
And strive with all that you are worth.

As from clay the potter can   (34)
Make whatever he wills—
So, in life, may every man
Reap as he sows and tills.

A gem, by chance, may lie before you,   (35)
And be gleaming in the rubble.
But fate won't pick it up for you—
It expects you to take that trouble.

Success always needs endeavour,   (36)
By wish alone it won't come near.
The jaws of sleeping lions never
Are visited by the passing deer.

Lessons well with parents done (37)
To excellence the offspring take;
Discharge from mother's womb alone
Will not the child a scholar make.

That mother was his enemy fated, (38)
That father an adversary,
By whom the child, left uneducated,
A goose midst swans will always be.

The scions of some noble line, (39)
With youth endowed, and beauty's powers,
But lacking learning, cannot shine:
They are no more than scentless flowers.

The fool may even look distinguished (40)
If dressed well, in Council Hall;
And this impression's not extinguished
As long he does not speak at all.'

Thinking thus, the king summoned an assembly of learned people. 'Listen, O savants', he said, 'is there at present any scholar among you who can teach policy and give a fresh lease of life to my sons, who have no learning, and are always going astray? For,

Set in gold, a piece of glass (41)
Can well assume the emerald's glow.
Similarly, the perfect ass
In company wise may learned grow.

'And, it is said,

The mind, my dear, in intercourse (42)
With lesser ones will degenerate;
With equals will not change, of course,

But improve greatly with the great.'

Then a great scholar named Viṣṇu Śarma, who knew the essence of all policy like Bṛhaspati himself, spoke up: 'Your Majesty, I will help these princes to learn policy, as they are from a noble stock. for,

No action can successful be   (43)
If expended on the unworthy.
As parakeets the stork cannot
Be made to speak, however taught.

'And, further,

A dullard born there cannot be   (44)
In such a noble family.
How could a piece of glass appear
In this mine of rubies rare?

'I will therefore make your sons expert in policy within six months.'

The king responded respectfully:

'Insects cling to flowers fine   (45)
And with them rise to crown's estate.
Stones too are honoured as divine
When set up by the good and great.

As objects on the hillside glow   (46)
By nearness to the rising sun,
The lowly glitter even so
With some good companion.

Worth is such for those who know it,   (47)
But fault for them who have no merit.
Fresh river water, a pleasant potion,

Turns undrinkable in the ocean.'

*S*aying, 'These sons of mine are therefore at Your Honour's disposal for instruction in the science of politics', the king then handed them over to Viṣṇu Śarma with all courtesies.

Mitralābha

Gaining Friends

After the princes were seated comfortably at the rear of the palace, Viṣṇu Śarma said to them by way of an introduction:

> 'The wise their moments spare will spend (1)
> In intellectual recreation.
> The foolish do that time expend
> In vice, or sleep, or recrimination.

'For the recreation of Your Highnesses, therefore, I will tell you the marvellous tale of the crow, the tortoise and the others.'

'Tell us, sir!' exclaimed the princes. 'Listen,' said Viṣṇu Śarma, 'now begins *Mitralābha* or the Gaining of Friends, of which this is the opening verse:

> Lacking means, of money bare, (2)
> But clever, and the best of friends:
> The crow and tortoise, mouse and deer,
> Did speedily attain their ends.'

'How did that happen?' asked the princes. Viṣṇu Śarma said:

There is a great silk-cotton tree by the side of the river Godāvari. Birds come there from all directions to roost at night. Once, as night was ending and the Lord of the Lilies,[1] the Moon, was about to set, a crow named Laghupatanaka or Quickflight woke up and saw a trapper drawing near, like Death personified. Observing him, the crow thought uneasily, 'The day has begun with an unlucky sight in the morning itself. Who knows what other disagreeable things this portends.' Deeply agitated, he followed the trapper, for

> Many a difficult situation, (3)
> Boding grief and full of fear,
> Afflicts the fool with no preparation,
> But not those who have taken care.

Furthermore, and this is a must for all those who seek the pleasures of life:

> Remember, as from bed you rise, (4)
> That mighty dangers lie in wait,
> Like illness, grief, your own demise:
> Today, who knows, which is your fate?

Meanwhile, the trapper had scattered grains of rice on the ground, spread out his net, and positioned himself in hiding. By and by, the bait was noticed by a king of the pigeons named Ćitragrīva or Spotted Throat, as he came cruising in the sky with his family. 'How is it possible,' he told the other pigeons who were tempted by the sight, 'that rice grains should lie scattered here in this desolate forest? We should first consider this. I do not see any good in it. The lure of this rice will lead us, in all probability, to the same fate as,

> The traveller who, from greed of gold, (5)
> In a muddy mire fell,
> And trapped there by the tiger old,
> Was killed and eaten, sad to tell.'

'How was that?' asked the pigeons. Their king recounted

The Traveller and the Tiger

*O*nce, when I was journeying through the southern forests, I saw an aged tiger by the side of a lake. Freshly bathed, he held some sacred *kuśa* grass in his paw as he cried out: 'O travellers, take this bracelet of gold!'

A traveller passing by was overcome by greed. 'This can only happen by a stroke of luck,' he reasoned to himself, 'but one should avoid actions involving personal risk. For,

> Even if misdeeds show profit, (6)
> The outcome cannot happy be.
> Nectar laced with poison in it
> Can only cause fatality.

'But then, every enterprise for making money is attended by risk. It is said,

> Good results no man can get (7)
> Without the risks of enterprise;
> But if on them he takes a bet,
> And survives, he'll surely rise.

So, let me first investigate this matter.'

'Where is your bracelet?' the traveller then demanded. The tiger stretched out his paw and displayed the ornament. 'But,' the traveller questioned him, 'how can I trust a murderous creature like you?'

'Listen, you wayfarer,' said the tiger, 'in the past, when I was young, I was indeed very wicked. I killed many men and cattle at that time. But now my wife and children are dead, and I have no family any more. A holy man instructed me to practice charity and other virtues; in accordance with that advice, I bathe and distribute alms. I have grown old, my fangs and claws have dropped. Why shouldn't I be trusted? For,

> Rituals holy, sacred study,   (8, 9)
> Doing penance, charity,
> Truth, forgiveness, fortitude,
> And not coveting: virtue's road
> With these eight, the scriptures say
> Is paved to form the righteous way.
> But, of these the first four go
> To often serve an outward show.
> The latter four alone can be
> In someone with true piety.

'As for me, I am now so far removed from worldly desires
that I wish to give away this golden bracelet, even though
it is on my own arm, to anyone at all. Even so, it is difficult
to dispel the slander that every tiger will prey on every man.
For,

> (Even though it be absurd,)   (10)
> People will follow the herd.
> In matters of religion, they
> Will accept the brahmin's say,
> Even though a cow he slay,
> Rather than the bawd's advice
> (No matter good, it smells of vice).

'I have studied all the scriptures. Listen:

> As to the desert, bringing rain,   (11)
> And to the famished, gifts of food,
> So to heal poverty's pain
> With charity, O prince, is good.

> As your life to you is dear,   (12)
> So is his to every creature.

The good, for all, compassion bear
By analogy with their own nature.

Of aye and nay, of pain and pleasure,　　　　　(13)
Of what may nice or nasty be,
Man can get the truest measure
By making self-analogy.

'And further,

As dirt, to see the wealth of others;　　　　　(14)
And wives of other men, as mothers;
In creatures all, yourself reflected:
Who sees thus is the man perfected.

'I can see that you are in a very bad way. I am therefore
trying to give you something. As the scriptures say,

Help the poor, O son of Kunti,　　　　　(15)
Do not to lords your money give.
What good is medicine for the healthy?
But the sick, by it, may live.

'And, further,

Given because it should be so done,　　　　　(16)
And not for sake of any return,
To one deserving, on right occasion:
Such gift is purest, you should learn.

'So have a bath in this lake, and take this bracelet made of
gold.'

Impelled by greed, the traveller believed what the tiger
had said. But as soon as he went into the lake to bathe, he
got trapped in the mud and was quite unable to escape.
'Oh! Oh!' said the tiger, seeing him stuck, 'You have fallen

into the mud-bank. I will pull you out.' Then, as the traveller
was by slow degrees approached and seized by the aged
animal, he reflected:

'To quote or not the sacred scripture,   (17)
Of virtue hardly is a sign.
That depends on basic nature:
By nature sweet is milk of kine.

'And,

Vain is indiscriminate action,   (18)
As washing of the elephant vain,[2]
As knowledge with no application,
As jewellery on the maiden plain.

'I did not do well to trust this murderer. It is well said,

Of clawed and hornéd creatures,   (19)
Of rivers and men who bear arms,
One should not trust their natures,
Nor of kings, or feminine charms.

'Further,

Judge each thing by its basic nature,   (20)
Less do other qualities matter.
Surpassing them without exception
Is innate predisposition.

'Besides,

Though sporting with the stars in heaven,   (21)
And piercing night with myriad rays,
The Moon himself, by fate's decree
Is swallowed by the Eclipse demon.

From your brow who can erase
What's writ there by your destiny?'

Thus lamenting, the traveller was killed and devoured by
the tiger.

~

'It is for this reason that I spoke about greed and gold. One
should never do anything without due consideration,' said
the king of the pigeons, 'for,

The grain well ripened,   (22)
The well-trained ward,
The wife well disciplined,
The well-served lord,
Well considered speech,
Deeds well understood:
For long will each
Give outcomes good.'

On hearing these words, one pigeon spoke up arrogantly:
'Ah! what a speech!

One may heed the words of old men   (23)
When an emergency meeting,
But thinking thus too long and often
Will leave no time for even eating.

'For,

If eating, drinking, everything,   (24)
Is on earth suspected,
How can then the carrying
On of life be here expected?

The folk to constant doubting prone,   (25)
To anger, hate or jealousy,
Those sullen or dependent grown:
These six must live in misery.'

Listening to him, all the pigeons alighted on the ground
baited with the rice grains. For,

Masters of the highest learning,   (26)
Whose doubts have fully been precluded:
Even they, the erudite and discerning,
Must suffer when by greed deluded.

And further,

From greed are born delusion,   (27)
Desire and chagrin.
Greed leads to sure destruction;
It is a cause of sin.

Furthermore,

Never was born a deer of gold,   (28)
Yet Rama coveted such a deer.
The mind, too, weakens, we are told,
When calamity is drawing near.

Meanwhile all the pigeons were trapped in the net. They
then began to berate the one at whose suggestion they had
come down. For,

In group work do not take the lead,   (29)
Its benefits will be equally shared.
But if the work does not succeed,
The one up front is never spared.

Spotted Throat heard their reproaches. 'It is not this pigeon's fault,' he said, 'for,

> When misfortunes are on their way,   (30)
> Friends too become the cause, they say:
> As when the buffalo calf is bound
> To restrict its liberty,
> Its own mother's leg is found
> A handy tethering post to be.

'And further,

> A friends is he, who from assault   (31)
> Of difficulties will rescue one,
> Not merely skilled in finding fault
> With what should or should not be done.

'To lose your wits at a time of trouble is itself a sign of cowardice. We must be courageous and think of a way out. For,

> Courage in calamity,   (32)
> Forgiveness in victory,
> In warfare chivalry,
> Eloquence in assembly,
> Love of reputation,
> To scriptures devotion:
> This is the true nature
> Of men of real stature.

> Not gleeful in prosperity,   (33)
> Nor downcast in adversity,
> Steady always in warfare:
> Rarely does a mother bear
> Such a son, from heaven sent
> To be the three worlds' ornament.

'And further,

> Six faults need avoidance: (34)
> Laziness and somnolence,
> Diffidence and anger,
> Procrastination, languor,
> By those who wish to do well
> In this world material.

'Now this is what we must do. In unison, we should lift up this net and fly away with it. For,

> The weak have successful proven   (35)
> When they join together;
> In a rope when grass is woven,
> It can the elephant tether.

> It's better to stay integrated   (36)
> With one's kin, though they be low.
> Rice, when from its husk separated
> Can never ripe and golden grow.'

After considering this, the pigeons lifted up the net together and flew away. The trapper saw them carrying it off from a distance, and ran after them, thinking,

> 'Together these birds fly away   (37)
> With my net; as soon as they
> Fall into disunity,
> Then in my power all will be.'

But he turned back once the birds had passed out of his sight. 'What should we do now?' asked the pigeons. Seeing that the trapper had gone. Spotted Throat said:

> 'By nature friends and parents care   (38)

For one's benefit and welfare,
But one must further reasons find
For others to be so inclined.

'In the Chitra forest on the banks of the river Gandaki, there
lives our friend Hiranyaka or Golden, a king of the mice.
He will cut this net off us.'

Reasoning thus, the pigeons proceeded to Golden's home.
The latter always feared the worst and lived in a burrow
with hundreds of passages. Terrified at the descent of the
birds, he stayed inside, still and silent.

'Comrade Golden,' Spotted Throat called out, 'why don't
you answer us?' Recognizing the voice, Golden came out
quickly. 'How lucky I am!' he cried, 'my dear friend Spotted
Throat has come here.

None can be more fortunate   (39)
Than one with opportunity
At a good friend's side to be,
And hold discourses intimate.'

But he was amazed to see all the birds enmeshed in the
net. 'Comrade, what is this?' he asked after a moment. 'This
is the result of our actions in a previous life, my friend,'
said Spotted Throat.

'In strict accordance with one's action,   (40)
Its nature and methodology,
The fruit is fated in proportion—
Good or bad as it may be.

Bondage, sickness, grief, afflictions,   (41)
Are fruit on trees of one's own actions.'

On hearing this, Golden rushed forward to sever Spotted
Throat's bonds. 'Not in this way, my friend,' said the king

of the pigeons, 'free these dependents of mine first. Then you may release me.'

'I am not so strong,' replied Golden, 'and my teeth are tender. How can I gnaw off the bonds of all these birds? I will remove you from the net if my teeth do not give way. After that I will deal with the others as best as I can.'

'All right,' Spotted Throat said, 'but use all your strength to set the others free.'

'Those who understand practical policy,' observed Golden, 'do not accept that dependents should be protected even at the cost of one's own life.

> For troubled times your money guard, (42)
> With all of it protect your wife.
> But wealth and wife, however hard,
> Spare not for saving your own life.

'Further,

> Virtue, pleasure, wealth, deliverance, (43)
> (the well-known fourfold human ends)
> All require life's existence,
> On its safety all depends.'

Spotted Throat said, 'Comrade, practical policy is indeed as you describe it. But I just cannot bear to see my dependents suffer. That is why I said what I did.

> For others should the wise abjure (44)
> Life and wealth, without a pause:
> Their termination is always sure;
> Better so for some good cause.

'There is also a special reason:

> These, my subjects, share with me (45)

Race, character, quality.
Now say, how else can fruitful be
The purpose of my sovereignty?

'Further,

They have not my side forsaken,   (46)
Even with no recompense.
You must save them, there's no question,
Even at my life's expense.

'And,

Friend, this body can't endure,   (47)
Its flesh and bone and filth: no more.
For it give up all consideration,
And only save my reputation.

'And furthermore,

This fleeting framework of pollution—   (48)
In its stead if one can gain
A pure and lasting reputation,
Friend, what does not one obtain?

'For,

Different, by far, is merit   (49)
From the frame corporeal:
One destructs within a minute,
The other for all time is real.'

Golden's hair bristled with delight as he listened to these words, 'Bravo! friend, bravo!' he cried, 'with such loving care for your subjects you are indeed fit to be a king, even of the three worlds.' He then bit off their bonds and, greeting

all of them with honours, added: 'Comrade Spotted Throat,
you should not blame yourself at all for any mistake in
getting caught in this net. For,

> The bird which can the carcass spot (50)
> From many miles above in air,
> When its time has come, will not
> See on ground the open snare.

'Furthermore,

> When the sun eclipsed I see, (51)
> And elephants wild in fettered state,
> And able men in poverty,
> I then realize how strong is fate.

'Further,

> Birds who roam the sky alone, (52)
> And denizens of the deepest sea,
> Both to getting caught are prone:
> How helpful can location be?
> What is a prudent policy?
> Time stretches out its deadly hand
> To seize one from the furthest land.'

After addressing Spotted Throat in this way, Golden
embraced him and did the duties of a host before seeing
him and his retinue off on their way home. He too then
returned to his burrow.

> Many friends of every mould, (53)
> To make, it is necessary.
> It was a friendly mouse, behold,
> Who gnawed the netted pigeons free.

Now Quickflight the crow was a witness to all that happened. 'O Golden,' he cried out with amazement, 'you are indeed praiseworthy. I too would like to be friends with you. Please favour me with your friendship.'

'Who are you?' Golden asked from inside the burrow. 'I am Quickflight the crow,' replied the other. Golden smiled and said, 'What friendship with you? For

In this world, the wise must see (54)
That those who come together
Should always be compatible.
How then can there be amity
With you, sir, the consumer
When I am the comestible?

'Furthermore,

Love between the prey and predator (55)
Leads only to catastrophe.
Deer, by Jackal trapped, was later
Helped by Crow to liberty.'

'How did that happen?' the crow asked. Golden narrated

The Deer, the Crow and the Jackal

There is a forest called Čampakavatī in the land of Magadha. In it there dwelt a deer and a crow who had been great friends for a long time. As the deer roamed about, sleek and well-fed, he was once noticed by a jackal who said to himself, 'Ah, how can I get to eat the fine flesh of this creature? Well, let me first win his confidence.'

After such cogitation, the jackal approached the deer and said: 'How are you, my friend?' 'Who are you?' the deer asked, and he responded, 'I am a jackal called Kṣudra-buddhi, that is Dimwit. I have no family and live like a ghost in this forest. Now that I have found you as a friend, I feel that I have come back once more into the world of the living with a brother. I will serve you in every way.' 'Very well,' the deer replied.

After the radiant and divine sun had set, they both proceeded to where the deer lived. His old friend Subuddhi or Goodwit the crow, also lived there on the branch of a champak tree. Seeing them, the crow asked: 'Comrade Ćitrānga, that is Spotted One, who is this with you?' 'This is a jackal,' said the deer, 'he has come, wishing to be our friend.'

'Comrade,' observed the crow, 'it is not appropriate to strike up a friendship with someone who has suddenly appeared out of nowhere. It is said:

The cat's misdemeanour   (56)
Caused the vulture's demise.
As such, say the wise,
Never give shelter
To one whose character
Or family ties
You cannot surmise.'

'How did that happen?' asked the other two animals. The crow narrated

The Cat and the Vulture

'On the hill called Gṛddhakuta by the side of the river Gangā there is a giant fig tree. In its hollow there lived a vul ure called Jaradgava or Eyeless. Ill luck had deprived him of eyes and claws. Taking pity on him, the other birds who lived on the same tree would give him some of their own food for his subsistence. In turn he used to guard their young.

Once a cat named Dīrghakarṇa or Longears came there with the intention of eating the young birds. The latter were terrified at seeing him draw near, and set up a great clamour, hearing which Eyeless called out, "Who comes here?" Longears saw the vulture and said fearfully to himself, "I am done for. But

> Danger one should always dread   (57)
> As long as it is far away.
> But once it is upon your head,
> Then face it in the proper way.

"Now it is impossible to run away from this vulture. So, be as it may, I will approach him and try to win his confidence." Having come to this conclusion, he went forward and said, "Sir, I salute you."

"Who are you?" asked the vulture.

"I am a cat."

"Go away. Otherwise I will kill you."

"Listen first to what I have to say," the cat responded, "then if I am to be killed, go ahead. For,

> Is mere race a sufficient reason   (58)
> For anyone to praise or murder;
> Not conduct, the criterion
> In deciding death or honour?"

"Tell me, then," asked the vulture, "why have you come here?" The cat said, "I am here on the bank of the Gaṅgā, observing the lunar fast, bathing daily and practicing celibacy. I have always been told by all trustworthy birds that Your Honour is devoted to virtue and knowledge. I therefore came to learn about virtue from someone who is hoary with knowledge. But you seem so virtuous that you are set to kill me, your guest. The householder's pious duty is thus described:

> From one who comes to cut it down, (59)
> Its shade withdraweth not the tree.
> So too should hospitality
> to even visiting foes be shown.

"In the absence of other means, a guest should at least be welcomed with loving words. For,

> A place to sit, a mat of straw, (60)
> Some water and a word of cheer—
> For every guest, at least these four
> In all good homes are ever there.

"Furthermore,

> For even those devoid of merit (61)
> The good always compassion bear.
> The moon does not its lustre limit
> In lighting up the outcaste's lair.

"Further,

> As priests to fire show veneration, (62)
> And other castes do priests revere,
> As wives for husbands have devotion,
> So guests are honoured everywhere.

> If a guest is turned aside (63)
> From your home, his hopes belied,
> Your merits stored he takes away—
> His own sins with you will stay.

"Further,

> If one base-born should visit you, (64)
> Even with your high-caste pride
> Give him all the honours due,
> For in the guest all gods reside."

"Cats like meat," said the vulture, "and little nestlings live here. That is why I said what I did." The cat remonstrated with horror, touching the ground and then his ears. "I have undertaken this difficult lunar fast," he said, "after studying the scriptures and giving up all attachments. The scriptures may differ among themselves, but they are unanimous that non-violence is the supreme virtue. For,

> All forms of violence who abjure, (65)
> Every temptation endure,
> To none deny a refuge sure—
> For them is open heaven's door.

> One friend alone will follow you (66)
> When you pass to death's dominion:
> It is the merit of your virtue—
> All else will perish with your person.

"Further,

> The difference is clear to see (67)
> When one's flesh is another's feast:
> Here a pleasure momentary,
> There loss of life at very least.

"Besides,

> The thought of certain death, in man (68)
> Engenders such agony—

By merely guessing no one can
Tell of its intensity.

"And listen again,

Sins tremendous why commit   (69)
For reasons of this wretched belly?
Fill it to the very limit
With herbs in forests growing freely."

Having thus assured the vulture, the cat began to live in
the same hollow in the tree. As time passed, he started to
catch the nestlings and bring them to the hollow where he
would devour them everyday. The birds whose young had
been thus consumed were distraught with grief. With loud
laments they searched for their children here and there.
Observing this, the cat slunk out of the hollow and ran
away. Meanwhile the birds found the remains of the nestlings
in that place. Concluding that Eyeless had eaten their young,
they killed the vulture.

~

'That is why,' continued the crow, 'I say that shelter should
never be given to one whose family and character are
unknown.' On hearing this the jackal retorted angrily: 'Sir,
your family and character too were unknown when the deer
first met you. How is it then that his affection for you
increased day after day?

Where there are no men of learning,   (70)
Even small minds are esteemed;
Like castor shrubs, without discerning,
In desert wastes as trees are deemed.

'Further,

> "This is mine, and this is not"—   (71)
> Thus do the small-minded see.
> The large-hearted have always thought
> The world itself a family.

'You too are my friend, just like this deer.'

'What is the point of this argument?' said the deer. 'Let us relax and continue our conversation at ease. For,

> No one is by nature   (72)
> Another's friend or foe.
> 'Tis conduct and behaviour
> Which always makes them so.'

'So be it,' agreed the crow, and each went his way in the morning.

One day the jackal told the deer privately, 'Comrade, there is a field full of corn in another part of the forest. I will take you there and show it to you.' This being done, the deer began to go to that field every day to feed on the corn. Eventually he was spotted by the farmer who set a trap for him.

On his next visit the deer was caught in the trap. 'Who but a friend,' he thought, 'can rescue me from this trapper's snare which feels like the noose of Death?' Meanwhile the jackal also came there and said to himself, 'The stratagem for getting what I want has finally succeeded. Once this deer is chopped up, I am bound to get some of the bones with a bit of the flesh and blood on them. That will give me plenty to eat.'

The deer was overjoyed to see the jackal. 'Comrade,' he exclaimed, 'cut me out of these bonds! Release me quickly! For,

In distress will you kinsmen know,   (73)
In debt the true, in war the brave;
The wife when money's running low,
And friends in emergencies grave.

'Furthermore,

Know him to be the comrade true,   (74)
In glee or gloom who stands by you,
In times of famine, anarchy,
In lawcourt and the cemetery.'

'He is good and caught,' thought the jackal, looking
repeatedly at the trap. 'Comrade,' he said, 'this snare is
made of animal sinew. How can I touch it with my teeth
today, when it is a sunday? Do not misunderstand me,
friend, but tomorrow morning I will do whatever you say.'
Then he hid himself nearby.

When the deer did not return home in the evening, the
crow went to search for him and found him trapped. 'What
is this, comrade?' he asked. 'This is the result of not listening
to a friend's advice,' replied the deer. 'It is said,

The man who will not lend his ear   (75)
To what well-wishing comrades say,
To misfortune is drawing near,
Gladdening enemies on the way.'

'Where is that cheat?' asked the crow. 'He is here,' replied
the deer, 'he is after my flesh.' The crow said, 'I had told
you so.

Saying, "it is no offence",   (76)
Cannot ground sufficient be
To trust the wicked. It makes sense
When virtue fears malignity.

Sure signals that your end is near: (77)
Snuffed-out lamps no odour bear
For you; nor can you sight
The morning star's receding light;
And words of friends you do not hear.

To you he speaks the loving word,   (78)
But stabs you when your back is turned:
Such a friend one must give up—
He's cream atop a poisoned cup.'

The crow sighed deeply. 'You fraud!' he exclaimed, 'what
dastardly deed have you done? For,

To sweetly entreat them,   (79)
And win them with your lying arts—
Is it good to cheat them,
Who come with hope and trusting hearts?

O Lady Earth, how can you bear   (80)
Upon your bosom those who dare
To treat with sinful treachery
Good, trusting, men of purity?

For villains, friendly inclination   (81)
Should be shunned: they are like brands
Which, heated, lead to conflagration,
And cold, will blacken still your hands.

'For this is the way of the wicked:

The villain is like the mosquito—   (82)
To your feet will he first go,
Then, fearless, on the back will bite
While singing gently all the night
Beside your ear. Once does he spy

A chance, he comes in suddenly.

Though the knave speak prettily,   (83)
To him your trust do not impart,
On his tongue may honey be,
But poison lies within his heart.'

At dawn the farmer came to the field, armed with a staff.
Seeing him, the crow said: 'Comrade deer, fill out your belly
with air, stiffen your legs and lie as if you are dead. When
I call out, you must get up and flee as fast as you can.'
The deer lay down as the crow advised.

The farmer beamed with joy when he saw the deer. 'Aha!
it has died on its own,' he said, as he released the animal
from the snare and started to gather up the ropes. Meanwhile
the deer heard the crow's call and swiftly got up and ran
away. The farmer hurled his staff after him and instead hit
and killed the jackal. It is said:

Here itself the consequence   (84)
Of deeds both really good or base,
The doer will experience
In three years, months, or even days.

'This is why,' concluded Golden, 'I said that love between
the prey and the predator can end only in disaster.'
The crow then said:

'For me to eat you, sir most fair,   (85)
Will not an adequate diet give.
But, like the pigeon, with you there
I too in safety hope to live.

'Further,

Even birds and beasts exhibit (86)
Mutual trust, if they have merit.
Never does good people's nature
Regress from its noble stature.

'Besides,

His mind is never agitated (87)
Though one may rouse a good man's ire.
Hardly will the sea be heated
By straw torches sputtering fire.'

'You are capricious,' said Golden. 'One should never make
friends with capricious people. It is said,

Bolder do some creatures grow (88)
The more trust on them you bestow.
This is mentioned of the crow,
The cat, the ram, the buffalo,
And of bad men, specially so.
Trust here is inappropriate, know.

'What is more, you, sir, belong to the category of our natural
enemies. It is said,

With enemies there can't be peace, (89)
No matter how well-made the pact.
Heat water as much as you please,
It puts out fire still, in fact.

The wicked always should be shunned, (90)
Even if with skills adorned.
Is the serpent's known menace
By jewelled hoods[3] made any less?

What can not, will never be, (91)

Nor otherwise, do understand.
An ox-cart will not cross the sea,
Nor ships move ever on the land.

If you think you can win over   (92)
Your foes, or an indifferent wife,
Just because you are in clover—
That's the end of your own life.'

Quickflight said, 'I have listened to all that you have said.
But I am determined to make friends with you. If not, I will
starve myself to death. For,

Friendships with the base remain   (93)
As pots made out of clay:
Easily shattered any day,
But hard to join again.
With good men, on the other hand,
They are like cups of gold:
Hard to spoil or splinter, and
Quick to mend or mould.

'What is more,

Melting points compatible   (94)
Make metals join together.
Sundry causes natural
Bring animals in tether.
The union of foolish men
Is due to greed and fear,
But of the noble only when
Perceptions they share.

'What's more,

As coconuts true friends appear   (95)

(Rough outside and sweet within).
The rest are like the jujube pear,
Their charm is only on the skin.

Though their friendships be no more,   (96)
Good people's values still endure.
Though blooms be cut from lotus stem,
Its fibres still adhere to them.

'Further,

Courage, devotion, courtesy,   (97)
Constancy in joy and grief,
Truth, sacrifice, integrity,
Are of friends the virtues chief.

'And, sir, where will I find one with such virtues, other
than yourself?'

After listening to the crow, Golden came out and said,
'Sir, I am overwhelmed by the nectar of your words. It is
said:

A bath with water cold and clear,   (98)
And sandal balm to soothe the flesh,
A garland of cool pearls to wear,
Cannot one stressed with heat refresh
As nicely as a good man's speech,
Full of loving words and wise,
Spellbinding incantations each,
Oft other good men gratifies.

'Further,

He can't keep secrets, importunes,   (99)
He's fickle, false, to anger given,
Gambles, cold in misfortunes,

A friend is blemished by these seven.

'You have not even one of the blemishes mentioned in this saying. For,

> While wit and veracity can (100)
> Be judged through mutual conversation,
> The dynamic but steady man
> Is only known by observation.

'Furthermore,

> Friendship of the spirits pure (101)
> Is always in a class apart.
> The words and actions different are
> Of those with villainy in the heart.

> The wicked always different are (102)
> In what they think, and do, and say;
> But thought and speech and action for
> The great-souled is a single way.'

'As you say, sir,' Golden concluded, 'so be it.' Making friends with the crow, he entertained him with a special repast and returned to his burrow. The crow too went home. From then onwards the two began to spend their time in exchanging gifts of food, enquiring about each other's welfare, and having other intimate conversations.

Once Quickflight said to Golden: 'Comrade, it is getting difficult to find food in this place, so I propose to leave it and go somewhere else.'

'Where can one go, friend?' asked Golden. 'It is said,

> One step will the wise man take (103)
> While holding back the other:
> Full inspection he should make

Ere quitting a place for another.'

'There is a place fully suitable,' said the crow. 'Which is that?' asked Golden. The crow replied, 'There is a lake called Karpura Gaura in the Daṇḍaka forest. An old and dear friend of mine lives there, a pious tortoise called Manthara, or Slow. For,

> Men find it easy to be clever   (104)
> In counselling others, it is seen.
> Great souls on their own duty ever
> Bent are few and far between.

'He will look after me with special things to eat.'
'Then why should I stay here?' cried Golden. 'For,

> Lands where you get no respect,   (105)
> Nor can livelihood expect,
> Or find knowledge, or have kin:
> They are not worth staying in.

> Livelihood and charity,   (106)
> A sense of shame and courtesy,
> Of the law a healthy fear:
> Where these five are just not there,
> In such a land your residence
> Should not be made (it makes no sense).

> Where these four lack, O comrade, never   (107)
> Should there one decide to live:
> A priest, a doctor, a good river,
> And someone who a loan will give.

Therefore take me there too.'
The crow then proceeded leisurely to the lake, chatting on a variety of subjects with his friend on the way. Slow,

the tortoise, saw them from a distance and, duly welcoming Quickflight, formally greeted the mouse as a guest. For,

At home whoever visits you   (108)
—Infant, youth, of aged station—
Respect to him is always due:
The guest, worldwide, gets veneration.

The crow said, 'Comrade Slow, this is Golden, a king of the mice. Give him special honours, for he is a pillar of virtue and an ocean of compassion. Even the king of the serpents, with his one thousand twin tongues,[4] may not be able to praise all his merits.' He then narrated the story of Spotted Throat. Slow, on his part, honoured Golden with all respect and asked: 'Good sir, be kind enough to say why you have come to this lonely forest.' 'I will,' said Golden, 'listen.' And he narrated

The Monks and the Mouse

There is a monastery in the city of Čampakā, in which there lived a monk called Čūdākarṇa. He used to beg for food and, after eating, would keep the leftovers in his begging bowl which he hung on a peg before going to sleep. I used to jump up and eat that food every day. Once a dear friend of Čūdākarṇa another monk called Vīṇākarṇa, happened to come there. While talking to him, Čūdākarṇa, kept beating the ground with an old piece of bamboo to scare me away. 'What is this, comrade?' Vīṇākarṇa asked. 'You appear disinterested in what I am saying, sir, and engrossed in something else.' Čūdākarṇa replied, 'Friend, I am not disinterested. But look at this mouse which troubles me. It always jumps up and eats the food kept in my begging bowl.'

Vīṇākarṇa stared at the peg. 'How can a mouse with little strength jump so high?' he said. 'There must be some reason for this. As it is said,

> When the wife is young and fair, (109)
> Whereas the husband aged is,
> And she draws him by the hair
> In tight embrace with sudden kiss—
> There must a reason be for this.'

'How could that be?' asked Ćūdākarṇa. Vīṇākarṇa narrated a tale.

The Old Man with a Young Wife

'In the province of Gauda there is a city called Kauśambi. In it there lived an exceedingly wealthy merchant named Ćandana Dāsa. He was in the evening of life, but lust filled his thoughts and, with the arrogance of riches, he married a merchant's daughter called Līlāvati. She was in the flush of youth, a veritable victory banner of the God of Love. The old husband gave her no satisfaction. For,

> As sun and moon give no respite (110)
> To those troubled by heat or cold,
> So women's hearts do not delight
> In husbands decrepit and old.

"Further,

> What passion can a man inspire, (111)
> With even hair gone grey and thin;
> Wives to others then aspire,
> While taking him as medicine.

"But the old man loved her deeply. For,

> For everyone, to live and earn (112)

Is a thing of great concern;
But, for one old, a youthful wife
Is dearer even than his life.

The old cannot indulge in pleasure   (113)
Nor give it up. Their only measure
Is the dog whose teeth have gone,
Merely licking at a bone.

"In time, Līlāvati overstepped the bounds of family honour with the pride of youth and fell in love with the son of a merchant. For,

Unrestrainéd liberty;   (114)
At father's home too long a stay;
Talks with men in assembly
Or out upon a festive day;
Living abroad; and company
Of ladies of low reputation;
Of proper conduct violation;
A husband prone to jealousy,
Or very old, or far away:
All are for women ruin's way.

"Further,

To drink and keep bad company,   (115)
To roam about excessively,
In others' homes to sleep, feel free
From husbands staying separately:
Six blemishes of women be.

When at a handsome man they stare,   (116)
A son or brother, though it were,
Women's private parts go wet,
Like an unbaked earthen pot

Whose bottom is all moist got
If water into it you let.

"What's more,

There is no ready time or place,　　　　　(117)
Nor man to make the loving plea—
That alone ensures, Your Grace,
In womenfolk their chastity.

Women, as the gods well know,　　　　　(118)
Have always very fickle been.
The men who guard them, even so
Are rather happy, it is seen.

To womenfolk, no man is dear　　　　　(119)
Nor displeasing, it is true:
Like cattle grazing forests bare,
They ever seek new grass to chew.

"Furthermore,

Woman is a ghee-filled jar,　　　　　(120)
And man is as a burning brand.
Fuel and fire never are
Together kept, please understand.

Not modesty, or training done,　　　　　(121)
Not diffidence or plain distaste—
The lack of suitors is alone
The cause of women staying chaste.

A child, she is her father's ward;　　　　　(122)
The husband's when she's in her prime;
The sons do her in old age guard;
She can't be free at any time.

"Once, as Līlāvati sat at ease on a bed dappled with the glint of serried gemstones, exchanging intimacies with the merchant's son, her husband arrived unexpectedly. Seeing him she sprang up at once and, drawing him by the hair, kissed and enveloped him in a long embrace. Her lover meanwhile ran away. It is said:

> The science, in which one expects (123)
> Celestial gurus most accomplished,
> Is by nature well established
> In all the feminine intellects.

"A professional bawd happened to be nearby. She observed the embrace, wondered at its suddenness, and got to know the reason. She then blackmailed Līlāvati in secret."

~

'That is why I spoke about the sudden behaviour of the young woman. Similarly, there is bound to be some reason for the energy of the mouse you have here,' said Vīṇākarṇa. Cūḍākarṇa thought for a moment, and said, 'The reason must be that there is a hoard of money here. For,

> In this life, always, everywhere, (124)
> It is the rich who power bear;
> Wealth is at the root, its certain,
> Even of the king's dominion.'

Then he took a spade and, digging up my burrow, seized the wealth which I had accumulated over a long time. After that I lost my energy and enthusiasm. I was unable even to forage for my own food. Cūḍākarṇa saw me cringing and crawling slowly, and said,

'Wealth gives in life a mighty stature,   (125)
With it one is both strong and wise;
Behold this mouse, a wretched creature,
Now reduced to proper size.'

'What's more,

As rivulets dry in summers hot,   (126)
So all the actions come to naught
Of persons who are indigent,
And also unintelligent.

'Furthermore,

With money one has many a friend,   (127)
And kinsmen too, one also can
On being hailed a sage depend:
One is then counted as a man.

'Further,

At home an emptiness descends   (128)
On one without a son or friends;
For fools all quarters empty ring;
But penury empties everything.

'Furthermore,

Unimpaired, and still the same   (129)
Are his senses, mind and name.
Yet, lacking the incandescence
Which derives from affluence,
In a moment man will change
Into someone else: it's strange.'

Hearing all this, I said to myself: 'It is not fitting for me to stay here now. Nor will it be appropriate to tell others what has happened. For,

> The wise accord no publicity, (130)
> To their losses monetary,
> To misdeeds in their family,
> To being duped, to humiliations,
> And to mental tribulations.

'Besides,

> One's age, and status monetary, (131)
> The secrets of the family,
> Favourite charms, and medications,
> Engaging in sex relations,
> Presents made or penance done,
> And humiliations undergone:
> All nine of these, one must beware,
> And keep concealed with every care.

'And it has been said,

> When luck turns bad on every side, (132)
> And effort will no more provide
> Results, despite one's fortitude:
> In such a difficult pass, where can
> The high-minded but poor man
> Find comfort, save in solitude?

'Further,

> The high-minded will rather die (133)
> Than to any meanness turn;
> As fire can extinguished lie,
> But never with a cold flame burn.

'What's more,

> As clusters of wild flowers do,   (134)
> The high-minded have but courses two:
> To be borne on every brow,
> Or wither on some forest bough.

'As to continuing to live here by begging, it will be extremely deplorable. For,

> Shorn of wealth, it is more meet   (135)
> To feed, with one's own life, the fire
> Funerary, than entreat
> Some ill-bred wretch (and risk his ire).

> Poverty engenders shame,   (136)
> And shame reduces confidence.
> The demoralized are easy game
> For contempt, which causes diffidence.
> There follows deep depression,
> Then loss of intelligence,
> Which leads to sure destruction:
> The root is indigence.

'What's more,

> Better is silence   (137)
> Than a falsehood said.
> Better is impotence
> Than another's wife in bed.
> Better a beggar
> Than to prosper on thieving.
> To die is far better
> Than in villains believing.

> Better keep an empty pen   (138)

Than a rogue bull inside.
Better wed a courtesan
Than a spoilt patrician bride.
Better live in wilderness
Than in a wayward ruler's land.
Better give up life, no less
Than to the base stretch out the hand.

'Besides,

As self-respect by servitude, (139)
And darkness by the moon's bright rays,
By course of age, all pulchritude,
By reading scriptures, sinful ways:
So, even though they be a host,
By begging are all virtues lost.

'Shall I then support myself with crumbs from another's table?' I thought to myself. 'Alas, that too is a second death.

Sex purchased with money spending, (140)
For food on others' grace depending,
Scholarship to trivials tied:
By all three are men mortified.

One sick, and long in exile grim, (141)
His bed and board on others' whim—
He lives a living death, and knows
In death alone he'll find repose.

'But I was greedy. Despite having considered all this, I decided to accumulate a store of wealth once again. It is said:

Greed affects one mentally. (142)
Cravings strong from it appear,

And they lead man to misery
Hereafter as well as here.

'Then Vīnākarṇa hit me with the old piece of bamboo as I
was crawling away slowly, and I thought: anyone who is
greedy nd discontented, for certain becomes his own enemy.
For,

Let the heart contented beat, (143)
And every riches will be thine.
To one with shoes upon his feet,
All earth is spread with leather fine.

'Furthermore,

Always running here and there (144)
Seeking money, can they find
That happiness which is the share
Of those who drink the elixir
Of contentment, peace of mind?

'What's more,

When one turns back from desires (145)
And to indifference aspires,
He has then all read and heard,
And put to practice every word.

'Besides,

Anyone who has no more (146)
To stand before a patron's gate,
Or pain of separation endure,
Or utter words importunate—
Consider his a blessed fate.

'For,

> Not far do million miles appear   (147)
> To those by cravings driven; and
> One contented does not care
> For even that which is at hand.

'As such it would be better to take a decision about what
is to be done in this situation.

> What is wisdom but decision,   (148)
> As virtue is for all compassion,
> And good health is the basic feature
> Of happiness in every creature.

'And so,

> Wisdom lies in firm decision   (149)
> When misfortunes arise;
> For those who tend to vacillation,
> At every step disaster lies.

'Similarly,

> The tribe comes first, before one man,   (150)
> And the village, before the clan.
> Forsake the village for the nation,
> But, for yourself, the whole creation.

'Furthermore,

> To drink plain water at one's ease,   (151)
> Or worrying, to eat delicacies:
> Having thought, I clearly see—
> In contentment lies felicity.

'After considering all this, I came here to this lonely forest. For,

> The forest has preferment: (152)
> Midst tiger wild and elephant,
> To live on fruit and water,
> With only trees for shelter,
> On leaves to sleep or rest,
> In bark alone be dressed;
> But not a life of poverty
> Midst relatives and family.

'Since then it has been my good fortune to be favoured by the love of this friend. That streak of luck has continued and, in Your Honour's company, I have found heaven itself. For,

> This worldly round, a poison tree, (153)
> Bears of sweet fruit only two:
> The nectar taste of poetry,
> And meeting people good and true.'

Slow said:

> 'As dust beneath the foot is wealth, (154)
> Youth races by, a mountain stream,
> A quivering drop, the body's health,
> And life a fleck of foam does seem.
> Wretched mind, which does not turn
> To dharma, key to heaven's door;
> In old age it will later burn
> With remorse and grief, for sure.

'You hoarded too much. This is the result. Listen,

> Money earned is better tended (155)

By using it for charity,
As water drained and thus expended
Keeps the tank from foulness free.

'Further,

Deeper as he digs the pit   (156)
To guard his gold by burying it,
The miser's hoard does lead as well
The way for him to go to hell.

'Further,

For his happiness not caring,   (157)
One who wants but wealth to earn:
Others' burdens he is bearing,
And only suffering in return.

'Furthermore,

Is it wealth, not spent nor gifted, which   (158)
Makes people to be counted rich?
Why, then even I and you
The selfsame wealth makes wealthy too.

'Further,

The miser's money, never spent,   (159)
Could be another's equally.
But losing it is such torment,
That it is his, it's plain to see.

These four are a rarity: (160)
Wisdom with no vanity,
Valour with magnanimity,
Wealth joined to renunciation,

And kindly words to each donation.

'And it is said,

Some hoarding one should always do,   (161)
But never take it to excess.
Look at the greedy jackal, who
By a bow was done to death.'

'How was that?' asked the other two. Slow recounted

The Greedy Jackal

In the district of Kalyāṇa there lived a hunter named Bhairava who once went to the Vindhyā forest looking for game. As he was returning, carrying a deer he had killed, he saw a great wild boar. He shot it with an arrow after putting the deer down on the ground. The boar too struck the hunter in the testicles with a terrible roar like a thunderclap, felling him like a tree. For,

Water, fire, poison, weapon,   (162)
Hunger, sickness, freaks of nature—
Encounter with such cause or reason
Separates life from every creature.

A snake was also killed by the thrashing of their feet. By and by, a jackal named Dīrgharava or Loudcry came wandering in search of food, and saw the deer and the hunter, the snake and the boar, all lying dead. 'O what a fine feast is here for me today,' he thought. 'Or rather,

Just as people are inflicted   (163)
With pains unthought of, even so
They meet with pleasures unexpected:
This is due to fate, I know.

'So be it. All this meat will last me comfortably for three months.

> For one month will the human last, (164)
> The deer and boar another two,
> The snake will break a single fast,
> But now, I'll eat the bow's sinew.

'So for my first meal, I will eat this tasteless cord strung on the bow.' Saying this, as Loudcry bit the string, the bow shaft leapt up and pierced his heart, killing him there and then.

~

'That is why I said that hoarding should not be taken to an excess. Similarly,' continued Slow,

> The rich man's wealth is that alone (165)
> Which he spends or gives away.
> With the rest, when he is gone,
> And with his wives, will others play.

'What's more,

> To worthy people what you give, (166)
> And that on which you daily live,
> That alone your wealth I merit:
> The rest you guard, others inherit.

'But let it be, what is the use of talking about the past? For,

> Those with clever minds do not (167)
> Hanker for what can't be got,

Nor lament for what is gone,
Or lose their calm when problems dawn.

'So, you must always persevere, comrade. For,

People study all of scripture   (168)
But still remain obtuse as ever.
He alone is learned, who
Puts learning into practice true.
Medicine though well made it be
The suffering patient cannot free
Of his ailment, just the same,
By mere taking of its name.

'Further,

The rules of science give no profit   (169)
To one who shies from application.
The blind may hold a lamp which is lit,
But do they have illumination?

'Therefore, comrade, you should come to terms with this
particular situation. And you should not consider it too hard.
For, it is the coward who says

Downfall from one's proper place   (170)
Always leads to loss of grace.
Of monarchs, specially, this is true,
Of clerics and ministers too,
And ladies with patrician air,
And even things, like teeth and hair,
Not to mention bosoms fair.

'And, knowing this, a sensible person should never move
from where he is. But,

Leaving their homes, far and near, (171)
Go lions, elephants, men of station.
Only cowards, crows and deer
Stay till death in the same location.

For men of courage and resolution, (172)
Which land is home, and which unknown?
By the prowess of their action,
Where'er they go, they make their own.
Like the lion, fanged and rampant,
The forest when he enters first,
There itself he slays the elephant
To drink its blood and quench his thirst.

'Furthermore,

As frogs to wells and tanks repair, (173)
And water birds to ample lakes,
So fortune, helpless as it were,
Its home in men of diligence makes.

'Further,

Pleasure, when it comes your way, (174)
Should be tended, as must pain.
Like the turning wheel will they
Come and go and come again.

'Further,

Prompt, and full of energy, (175)
In new skills versed and precepts old,
From vices and addictions free,
Grateful, firm in friendship, bold:
Herself the goddess of all riches
Comes to live with one who such is.

'And, specially,

A hero touches heights of glory,   (176)
Of wealth though he may have no aid;
No honour in the miser's story
Even though of money made.
Behold the lion's inborn glow,
Of massed merits the domain.
Can a dog that lustre show,
Though it wear a golden chain?

Why so proud you're rich today,   (177)
And lament when wealth has flown?
Men are like a ball in play:
Struck, it bounces up and down.

'Furthermore,

As the passing cloud's cool shade,   (178)
Young maids, new rice, false amity,
Are youth and wealth of such stuff made:
Their savour is but transitory.

The Maker also helps you live—   (179)
For this, too hard you need not strive.
When from the womb a child appears,
Its milk the mother also bears.

'Indeed, comrade,

He, by whom were swans created   (180)
White, the parrots emerald green,
And peacocks' plumage variegated,
Your sustenance He will ordain.

'Furthermore, comrade, listen to a secret kept by good people:

Wealth causes pain in acquisition,   (181)
In troubled times, anxiety,
In affluence some strange delusion,
Can it a cause for comfort be?

'Furthermore,

In seeking wealth for causes good,   (182)
Indifference is the better way.
Instead of cleaning stains of mud,
Better far from mud to stay.

'For,

The prey of beasts is on the land,   (183)
And of birds in realms of air,
The fish find theirs in water, and
The rich are preyed on everywhere.

As with death all living things,   (184)
The wealthy live in constant fear
Of flood and fire, thieves and kings,
And even of their kinsmen near.

'Similarly,

In this life, so full of care,   (185)
There is no greater misery:
The wealth you yearn for is not there,
Nor are you from yearnings free.

'And, brother, listen further,

First, wealth is difficult to obtain,   (186)
Guarding it is then a strain,
Losing it is like death, a bit,

Better not to think of it.

Craving when you set aside,   (187)
Then who are masters, who the poor?
But to it access once provide,
And servitude is at your door.

'Furthermore,

Whatever one longs for, indeed,   (188)
New longings will in turn succeed.
So, get that by which the need
Itself of longing will recede.

'What more is there to say? Be my friend, and spend your
time here with me. For,

In great souls, love till death abides,   (189)
And wrath within moments subsides.
While giving they are always free
Of thoughts of reciprocity.'

On hearing this, Quickflight said: 'Bless you, Slow, your
merits deserve to be praised for ever. For,

The good alone have ability   (190)
To save good men in difficulty.
bogged in mud do elephants need
Other elephants to get them freed.

Of all the people on this earth   (191)
True praise is due to him alone,
That best, that blessed man of worth
From whose door not anyone
Who sought refuge or supplicated
Was turned away, his hopes frustrated.'

In this way they lived happily, content with feeding and enjoying themselves as they pleased.

One day a deer named Citrānga or Dapplebody, who had been frightened by someone, came there and met them. Considering that whatever had scared him might be coming after him, Slow went into the water and the mouse entered his burrow. The crow also flew away and perched on top of a tree, from where he looked far and wide but could not see anything to be afraid of. On his word the rest came back and they all sat down together.

'Very well,' said Slow, 'deer, you are welcome. Eat and drink as you please, and favour this forest by staying here.'

Dapplebody replied: 'A hunter scared me. I have come to Your Honours for refuge, and I would like to have your friendship.'

'That you have got even without trying,' said Golden, 'for,

Of friendship, know, four kinds there be: (192)
Those based on blood, then family,
And on traditions hereditary,
Or help in some calamity.

'Your Honour should therefore stay here and regard this place as your own home.'

The deer was delighted at hearing this and, having eaten and drunk his fill, he sat down in the shade of a tree by the water. 'Comrade deer,' said Slow after some time, 'what frightened you in this desolate forest? Is it that there are hunters moving about?'

The deer said: 'In the land of Kalinga there is a monarch named Rukmāngada. He has come in the course of a conquering expedition and is at present encamped with his army on the banks of the river Candrabhāgā. A rumour among the hunters has it that he will come here in the morning and is bound to be by the lake Karpūra. As such, considering that our stay here will also be endangered in the morning, we should start taking appropriate steps.'

On hearing this the tortoise said fearfully: 'I will go to another lake.' The crow and the deer said, 'Very well,' but Golden observed with a smile: 'All will be well for Slow once he gets to another lake. But what can he do while moving on land? For,

> In water lies the fish's power,   (193)
> And of beasts in their domain,
> Of castellans in wall and tower,
> Of kings in their ministers main.

'Comrade Quickflight, with such advice, what is bound to happen is,

> To see his young bride's budding breast   (194)
> By another kissed and pressed,
> As the merchant's son was peeved,
> Even so will you be grieved.

'How did that happen?' they asked. Golden began a story.

The Merchant's Bride

*I*n the land of Kānyakubja there was a king named Vīrasena. He appointed a prince by the name of Tungabala as the governor of the city of Vīrapura. As this exceedingly wealthy young man was going around his city, he happened to see a merchant's daughter-in-law named Lāvaṇyavatī, who was in the full bloom of youth. Smitten by desire, he returned to his palace and sent a messenger woman to her. For,

> Till then only man does stay   (195)
> On the course of virtue's way,
> Keep his urges in control,

Of shame and decorum, know the role:
Until, from brows drawn to the ear
The arrow of some wanton glance
Released, dark-winged, his heart will tear,
And rob him of his resistance.

Lāvaṇyavatī too could think of nothing else from the moment
she saw him, for her heart had also been struck and shattered
by love's arrows. As it is said:

Falsehood, wile and reckless daring,   (196)
Greed and envy overbearing,
No merits, much impurity,
Are faults innate in femininity.

After listening to the messenger woman, Lāvaṇyavati said:
'I am a faithful wife. How can I commit this sin of betraying
my husband? For,

A woman with all skills domestic,   (197)
Who loves her husband as her life.
In bearing children most prolific,
And always chaste—such is the wife.

The name of "wife" should be denied   (198)
To one who can't her husband please.
The latter being satisfied,
The gods with women are at ease.

'Therefore, whatever the lord of my life commands, that I
will do without demur.'

'Is that truly so?' asked the messenger woman.
'Absolutely,' Lāvaṇyavati replied. The messenger then went
and conveyed all this to Tungabala. 'How is it possible,' he
cried, 'that her husband will bring her here and hand her
over to me?' The messenger observed, 'An expedient must

be worked out. As it has been said,

> The jackal, on a muddy course,   (199)
> Did slay the mighty elephant.
> What cannot be done by force,
> Needs doing by expedient.'

'How did that happen?' asked the prince. The messenger woman related

The Elephant and the Jackal

'There was an elephant called Karpūratilaka or Camphorhead in the forest of Brahmāraṇya. Observing him, all the jackals used to think, "If this one were to die by some means, his carcass would enable us to eat at will for four months." An old jackal there declared, "I will ensure his death by applying my intelligence." Then that rascal approached Camphorhead and, saluting him with an eightfold prostration, said, "Lord, favour me with a glance."

"Who are you?" asked the elephant. "From where have you come?"

"I am a jackal," he replied, "sent to Your Honour by all the animals of the forest after they met together. As it is not proper to live without a king, Your Honour has been chosen for consecration to the monarchy of this forest as possessed of all the royal qualities. For,

> One who is immaculate   (200)
> In conduct, birth and family,
> Skilful in affairs of state,
> Of known prowess and piety—
> It is fit that such a person
> On the earth should have dominion.

"Furthermore,

One must first a king obtain,   (201)
Then money and the bridal hand;
For how can wife and wealth remain
Without a ruler in the land?

"Further,

Kings support to people give,   (202)
Like clouds which bring the monsoon shower.
Though rains may fail, the people live,
But not when kingdoms lose their power.

"What is more,

In some thrall is all mankind—   (203)
Good natures here are hard to find.
If someone to the law adheres,
It's often punishment he fears.
When women of good family
Cohabit in great penury
With husbands sick or maimed or mean,
They fear punishment, it is seen."

The jackal then got up and went away, saying, "Lord, please
come quickly so that the auspicious moment for the
coronation is not lost."

Surrendering to greed, Camphorhead ran along the path
by which the jackal had gone, and fell into a great mudbank.
"Comrade jackal," he then cried out, "what should I do
now? I have fallen into the mudbank and will die! Come
back and see!"

"Lord," the jackal said with a smile, 'hold my tail, and
get up. As you gave credence to the word of one like myself,
you must suffer the painful consequence from which there
is no way out. As it is said,

With the good if you will be,   (204)
You will have prosperity.
But fall into bad company,
And fall you will then certainly."

Drowned in the mudbank, the elephant was then devoured
by the jackals. It is for this reason that I spoke about what
can be done by expedients.'

~

In accordance with the messenger woman's advice the prince
appointed the merchant's son, whose name was Ćaru Datta,
as an attendant, and engaged him in all his confidential
affairs.

One day, after the prince had bathed, made his toilet
and put on ornaments of gems and gold, he declared to
Ćaru Datta, 'Starting from today, I will observe the religious
rite[5] of the goddess Gauri for a month. You must therefore
bring a young woman of good family here every night, and
present her for worship by me with the proper rituals.'

Ćaru Datta began to bring and hand over a damsel as
he had been directed. But he would then hide and see what
the prince did with her. And Tungabala, without even
touching the young woman, would offer worship to her from
a distance with garments, ornaments and cosmetics, and
send her away with the guard.

The merchant's son became confident about what he had
seen. His mind full of cupidity, he brought his own bride
Lāvaṇyavatī and presented her one night. Tungabala
recognized his heart's beloved. Getting up eagerly, he took
her in his arms and, with eyes closed in ecstasy, made love
to her on the bed. The merchant's son was deeply distressed
to see this. But he did not know what to do, and could
only stand like a figure painted in a picture.

'This is why I talked about seeing the bride and so on. You will also go the same way,' said Golden.

Slow ignored the good advice. Distraught, as it were, with a great fear, he abandoned the lake and walked away. Golden and the others followed him, fearing the worst because of their love for him. As he moved along the ground, he was spotted by a hunter who was roaming in the forest. The hunter seized him and, picking him up, tied him to his bow. Then he proceeded homewards, tired from travelling and troubled by hunger and thirst.

The deer, the crow and the mouse followed the hunter in deep despair. Golden lamented:

'The ocean of one misfortune (205)
I had not crossed, when all too soon
A second have I now come by:
One slip, and troubles multiply.

It's luck alone, that there can be (206)
One, who by nature is your friend.
Such friendship, of all pretence free,
In troubles even does not end.

Such trust can people never share (207)
With mother, sibling, spouse, or son,
As the confidence they bear
A friend who is by nature one.'

He fretted again and again: 'How unfortunate am I! For,

In this one life itself I see (208)
Such situations, full of change

Both good and bad, which times decree
To flow out from the spreading range
Of my own deeds as, in a sense,
Is many lives' experience.

'And this too is true,

Dangers near this body hide,   (209)
Troubles in all wealth reside.
Parting follows every meeting,
All creation is so fleeting.'

On further reflection, he said,

'From foes, and fear and grief protecting,   (210)
Your pleasures and your trust respecting,
Who coined this word, this apothegm
Called "friend" which is, in fact, a gem.

'What is more,

For eyes a salve of pleasure pure,   (211)
Ever delightful to the mind,
In joy and grief a partner sure,
Such a friend is hard to find.
Others one meets everywhere,
Fair-weather friends, for money yearning.
For judging if they are sincere,
The touchstone is a crisis burning.'

After lamenting thus for long, Golden said to Dapplebody
and Quickflight, 'An effort must be made to rescue Slow
before the hunter comes out of the forest.'

'Tell us quickly what to do,' said the other two. Golden
replied, 'Let Dapplebody go near the water and pretend to
be dead. The crow should sit upon him and peck at him

with his beak. This hunter will certainly drop the tortoise and go in haste for the deer's flesh. I will then bite off Slow's bonds, and you both should flee as the hunter approaches you.'

Dapplebody and Quickflight immediately did as they had been told. The tired hunter drank some water and sat down under a tree. Then he saw the deer and went towards it happily with a knife. Meanwhile Golden came and bit off Slow's bonds, and the tortoise swiftly entered the lake. The deer, seeing the hunter approach him, jumped up and fled.

When the hunter returned to the foot of the tree and saw that the tortoise was no longer there, he said to himself: 'I deserve this for my carelessness. For,

> Who some certain gain forsaking,   (212)
> To one uncertain giveth chase—
> The former's loss he's definite making,
> The other's lost in any case.'

And he returned to his camp, disappointed because of his own actions. As for Slow and the others, freed from their worries, they went home where they lived happily.

~

'We have listened to all of this,' said the princes joyfully, 'and we are delighted. We have got what we wanted.' Viṣṇu Śarma replied: 'What Your Highnesses desired so far has been accomplished. May there be this too:

> May all good people find a friend,   (213)
> And the country prosper fair.
> May kings this earth guard end to end,
> And ever firm their duty bear.
> May your hearts be satisfied

By science of good government,
As by a newly wedded bride.
And by the god whose ornament
Is the moon upon his crest,
May all the people here be bles't.'

Suhrdbheda

Splitting Partners

'*N*oble sir,' said the princes, 'we have well understood your lesson about the gaining of friends. Now we would like to learn the splitting of partners.'

'Listen then,' replied Viṣṇu Śarma, 'to *Suhṛdbheda* or the Splitting of Partners, of which this is the first stanza:

In the forest, growing full,   (1)
The lion's friendship with the bull
Was by the greed and villainy
Of a jackal ruined utterly.'

'How did that happen?' asked the princes. Viṣṇu Śarma said:

*I*n the southern region there is a city called Suvarṇavati. A merchant named Vardhamāna lived there. Even though he was very rich, seeing that his other relatives were even richer, he decided that he must further increase his wealth. For,

Whose sense of greatness does not grow   (2)
While looking at those down below?
But all who upwards their sights raise
Feel small and poor with every gaze.

The man of wealth is highly prized,   (3)
Although he may kill a priest,

A brahmin at the very least.
But one who is in penury,
Though of the noblest pedigree,
Is nevertheless despised.

Further,

The goddess of prosperity (4)
Does not care to give her favours
To one who has no industry,
Is lazy, lacking in endeavours,
A fatalist; just like the maid
To a husband old and staid.

What is more,

Six qualities which do impede (5)
To greatness those who would proceed,
Are: being duped by feminine grace,
Too partial to one's native place,
Idle, sickly, diffident
And, with what one has, content.

For,

Even little wealth when one (6)
Considers as a treasure store,
Then fate, I think, for him has done
What it could, and does no more.

Furthermore,

Lacking valour and endeavour, (7)
For enemies a source of joy,
Mirthless: may no mother ever
Proffer birth to such a boy.

As it has been said,

> You should always want to get (8)
> Something you don't have as yet;
> And when you get it, guard it so
> That it will continue to grow.
> And once it has grown, as it may—
> To those deserving give it away.

For, if one does not wish for something one does not have, one will never get it for lack of effort. And what one has, even if it be a great treasure, will deplete by itself unless it is safeguarded. Besides, wealth which does not appreciate will decay in course of time, like kohl for the eyes even though it be used sparingly; and if wealth is not to be enjoyed, it just has no purpose. As it has been said:

> Wealth not used for charity, (9)
> Or enjoyed as it should be;
> Strength by which the enemy
> Is not put into jeopardy;
> Learning of the sacred writ
> If one does not practice it;
> And the self which can't control
> Its senses and its passions' role:
> What with these is there to do?
> (They do not serve their purpose true.)

Further,

> (With the passing of days) (10)
> See, how collyrium decays
> And the ants their towers raise.
> Let your time productive be
> With study, work and charity.

For,

> As drops of water, one by one, (11)
> Fill the pitcher, so is done
> The aggregation, bit by bit,
> Of knowledge, wealth and holy merit.

> The man whose days pass vacantly— (12)
> He does not spend, nor does he give:
> Like the blacksmith's bellows, he
> Breathes indeed, but does not live.

Thinking thus, he yoked two bulls named Nandaka or Joyful, and Sanjivaka or Lively, to a cart and, filling it with all manner of merchandise, set out for trading towards Kashmir.

> What burden is too much or great (13)
> For those of strong and able state?
> What destination is too far
> For those who enterprising are?
> Which country is a foreign land
> For those equipped with knowledge? And
> Who can be the enemy
> Of those who will speak lovingly?

As they passed through a great forest called Sudurga, Lively fell down and broke a knee. Observing him, Vardhamāna said to himself:

> 'One well versed in policy (14)
> May make his efforts here and there,
> But their fruit will always be
> Such as providence does bear.

'But,

Indecision is utterly   (15)
To be shunned, as it will be
An obstacle in every action.
So, leave aside all vacillation,
And make an effort so may you
Accomplish what you want to do.'

After reflecting in this way, Vardhamāna abandoned Lively there and himself went to the town of Dharmapura from where he procured another big bull and, yoking it to the cart, continued his journey. As for Lively, somehow he balanced himself on three hooves and got up. For,

In deepest ocean you may dive,   (16)
By snakes be stung, or fall from hill;
Yet if you have more time to live,
Then fate will guard your vitals still.

No creature dies before its turn   (17)
Though pierced by scores of arrows stern.
Yet merely touched with softest clover,
It lives not if its time is over.

When one has fate in his defence,   (18)
Then he may stand without protection.
But, targeted by providence,
Though guarded he will meet destruction.
The orphan in the forest cast,
Lives; at home he may not last.

As the days passed, Lively wandered about the forest, feeding and frolicking as he pleased. He became sleek and stout, and let forth loud bellows. In that forest there also lived a lion called Pingalaka or Tawny, enjoying the comforts of a domain he had acquired by the force of his own arms. As it has been said:

The lion's crowning, formally,   (19)
By other beasts is never done.
Self-evident is his sovereignty
In kingdoms by his prowess won.

Once the lion was thirsty, and went to the bank of the
Yamuna to drink water. There he heard Lively bellowing. It
was like the roll of thunder out of season, something he
had never experienced before. Startled, he turned back
without drinking. On getting home, he stood silently,
wondering what it could have been.

In that condition he was noticed by Karataka or Rusty
and Damanaka, or Bossy, two jackals who were the sons of
his ministers. Seeing him thus, Bossy said to Rusty: 'Comrade
Rusty, why is it that our master does not drink water though
he is thirsty, but stands there looking alarmed and bemused?'

'Friend Bossy,' replied Rusty, 'in my opinion there is no
need at all to pay attention to the master. What do we have
to do with enquiring about his activities? For we have long
been ignored by this king, and have suffered greatly for no
fault of ours.

See what must all servants do   (20)
For sake of money when they serve.
The freedom of their person too,
Then the fools cannot preserve.

'Furthermore,

Of cold and heat and wind, the pain   (21)
That those who others serve must bear,
A fraction of that, borne in prayer,
For the wise could heaven gain.

'Further,

Life is worthwhile insofar (22)
As it is in freedom led.
As for those who vassals are,
They live, but are no more than dead.

'Furthermore,

Come here, go out, sit, stand and stay, (23)
Be silent, speak: and even so
Do the rich with servants play,
Who, gripped by hope, to them do go.

Fools, for wealth and profit's sake, (24)
Like a whore their persons preen,
And of themselves, for others, make
An implement, a mere machine.

'What is more,

Though fickle be the master's gaze, (25)
Bestowed even on the base,
Even so, do servants deem
It as a mark of high esteem.

'Furthermore,

Thought stupid, if he silent stays, (26)
A windbag, if in speech fluent;
Timorous, if with patient ways,
And ill-bred, if too recusant;
Saucy, if he stands too near,
A laggard, if he stays afar:
Sages too can't make them clear—
The servant's tasks so complex are.

'And, especially,

He bows and scrapes to get a rise,   (27)
And kills himself to make a living.
Who but the serf is so unwise—
For pleasure, pain to himself giving.'

Bossy said: 'You should never even think like this. For,

Kings and lords, when satisfied,   (28)
Are quick your wishes to fulfil.
Why indeed should one deride
Serving them with care and will?

'See further,

Leaving royal service, where   (29)
Can servitors those benefits gain
Which come with fans and sunshades fair,
With horse and elephant in one's train?'

'Even so,' replied Rusty, 'what do we have to do with this matter? One should always desist from getting involved in matters that do not concern one. Look,

One who to interfere will try   (30)
With things he has no business in,
On the floor, dead, he will lie,
Like the ape who pulled the pin.'

'How did that happen?' asked Bossy. Rusty narrated

The Meddlesome Monkey

A scribe named Śubha Datta had begun to build a monastery on some land near a sacred forest in the Magadha country. A beam being used for the work had been sawn only in part, and the carpenter had placed a pin between the two pieces of wood. A large troop of monkeys happened to come there while playing about. One ape, as if inspired by death, sat down with his hands on the pin, while his genitals dangled between the two half-split pieces of timber. With natural restlessness, he then pulled out the pin after a great deal of effort. And, as the pin came out, his testicles were crushed and he died.'

~

'That is why I talked about not interfering,' concluded Rusty. 'Nevertheless,' said Bossy, 'it is essential for servants to observe their master's activities with care.' Rusty responded: 'Let the Prime Minister do it. He is appointed to be in charge of everything. A servant must never interfere in the business of others. Look,

> For the master's sake to interfere (31)
> In things which are not one's affair,
> Causes grief, as was the case
> Of the ass belaboured for his brays.'

'How did that happen?' asked Bossy. Rusty recounted

The Intrusive Ass

*I*n Varanasi there was a washerman named Karpūra Paṭaka. Once, after having made love to his young bride for a long time, he fell into a deep sleep in her arms. A thief then entered the house to steal the goods inside. At that time an ass was tethered in the washerman's courtyard, and a dog lay on the floor.

'Comrade,' said the ass to the dog, 'this is really your business. Why don't you make a commotion and wake up the master?'

'Good sir,' replied the hound, 'you must not interfere in my affairs. Don't you know that I guard the master's house night and day? But he has been free of care for so long that he does not realize any more how useful I am and now pays little attention to feeding me. Indeed, masters pay little attention to servants until they have problems.'

'Listen, you blockhead,' said the donkey.

Is he a servant true indeed   (32)
Who makes demands in times of need?'

'Listen indeed!' retorted the dog, 'And what about the master who is kind only when there's need of you? For

Serving a master,   (33)
Or looking after
Servants with grace,
As in the case
Of practicing religion,
Or begetting a son,
Cannot be done
By proxies for one.'

'You wretch!' cried the ass in a rage, 'are you so wicked that you will neglect your master's affairs when there is an emergency? Well, so be it. I must do what I can to wake the master up. For,

The sun's warmth cherish on the back,   (34)
The fire's on your nether part,
With guileless tread, sweet heaven's track,
And the master's work with all your heart.'

Saying this, he began to bray with all his might. The washerman was awakened by his screams. Incensed at his sleep having been disturbed, he got up and thrashed the ass with a stick.

~

'That is why I talk about not interfering in other's affairs,' said Rusty. 'Look. We have been appointed only to scout for game. Let us do our own work. On further thought, there is no need to do even that today. For there is plenty of food left over from what we have eaten.'

'How can you serve the king only for the sake of food?' asked Bossy angrily. 'This is unworthy of you. For,

Wise men royal service chose   (35)
To help their friends and harm their foes.
This was their true reason, really,
For who cannot just fill his belly?

That life is successful indeed,   (36)
Whose living also helps to feed
The priest, the friend, the relative:
For who does not for himself live?

'Besides,

He truly lives, he does indeed,   (37)
By whose life many will be living.
Their own selves even crows can feed,
From beak to belly morsels giving.

'Look,

One man, for silver pieces five,   (38)
Will servitude accept, for sure.
Others for a thousand strive,

Some can't be had for even more.

'Further,

When humankind is all the same, (39)
Servitude's a mark of shame.
There too, if one lacks primacy,
It's better dead that he should be.

'And it is said.

The differences are great indeed (40)
In elephants and in types of steed;
In metals, timbers, and in stone;
In women, men, and garments worn.
In waters too, the difference,
As with the rest, is quite immense.
(Everything as one may see,
Has its own peculiarity.)

'Similarly,

Even with a bit of bone, (41)
Foul with scraps of gut and grease,
Meat upon it having none,
For his hunger to appease,
The dog is all the same content.
But the lion will, in turn,
In his grasp the jackal spurn,
And slay instead an elephant.
In distress even, every creature
Seeks that which matches its own nature.

'Furthermore, look at the difference between one who is just
a servant by nature, and one who is worthy of being served:

The dog will wag his tail, and go (42)
Grovelling down, his belly show
Before his feeder; but the brave
Elephant gazes long and grave
At the hand which offers bread,
And must be coaxed, before he's fed.

'What is more,

A life which is well known to be (43)
Of learning, fame and bravery,
Though even of a moment's span,
It is truly lived by man.
For even crows can long survive
By eating scraps to stay alive.

'Furthermore,

One who lacks compassion for (44)
Children, elders, slaves, the poor,
And kinsfolk: in this sphere mundane,
What fruit does his existence gain?
For, even crows can long survive
By eating scraps to stay alive.

'And even further,

'Twixt good and bad he can't discern, (45)
The scriptures he does mostly spurn,
His only wish is for a feast:
Is he better than a beast?'

'But we are subordinates,' said Rusty. 'What do we have to
do with such considerations?' Bossy replied. 'How long does
it take for advisers to be promoted and not remain
subordinates? For,

By nature none show benefaction,   (46)
Be villainous to or sympathize
With another. It's his action
Which exalts man or otherwise.

'What is more,

Great effort must be made to haul   (47)
A heavy boulder up a hill,
But down to let it slip and fall
Is a moment's matter still.
The same it is for man in case
Of treading good or sinful ways.

By his actions man does go   (48)
To greater heights, or sink below:
Like one who builds a tower fine,
Or the digger of a mine.

Therefore, good sir, everyone's place depends upon his own efforts.' 'Well then,' asked Rusty, 'what is it that you want to say?'

'This master of ours, Tawny, is scared for some reason. He has just been sitting since he returned,' the other replied.

'Do you know what has happened?' asked Rusty. 'What is so mysterious here?' observed Bossy. 'It is said,

Even beasts can understand   (49)
Meanings put in language clear.
When they are ordered, horses and
Elephants quick their burdens bear.
But clever people can infer
Also that which is unsaid:
To know what other hearts prefer
Needs but a perspicacious head.

What there is inside the mind (50)
Can from the features be divined,
From gestures, motions, efforts, speech,
And eye and facial changes each.

'So I will use my head and build close relations with the
master at this time of anxiety. For,

Words befitting the occasion, (51)
And courtesies suiting the intention,
And wrath which can be matched by deed:
Who knows all this is wise indeed.'

Rusty said: 'Comrade, you do not know the ways of service.
Look,

Such a one has lost all wit, (52)
Who, thinking he's the king's favourite,
Comes without an invitation,
And then, unasked, makes much oration.'

'Good sir,' said Bossy, 'how can it be said that I do not
know the ways of service? Look,

Is a thing by very nature (53)
Beautiful or otherwise?
Whatever pleases any creature
Is full of beauty to its eyes.

'For,

Whatever be one's disposition, (54)
Through it, the wise, by insinuation
Will quickly establish a role
And take him into their control.

'Further,

"Is there anyone at hand?" (55)
"'Tis I, for you to please command."
Thus replying to the king,
The servant should then quickly bring
With the best of his exertion
The royal order to fruition.

'Furthermore,

One should with the king reside— (56)
Who's steadfast, wise and temperate,
Like a shadow, always at his side,
And ordered, who won't hesitate.'

'Perhaps the master will deride you for coming without a proper occasion,' observed Rusty. 'So be it,' the other replied, 'but it is still necessary for a servant to present himself before the master. For,

Not starting, for he fears to make (57)
An error, is the coward's sign:
For fear of getting stomach-ache,
Will, my dear, one never dine?

'Look,

The man in his proximity, (58)
The king will favour, though he be
Unread, base, or unworthy.
For kings and damsels, generally,
Like creepers, tend to cling to that
Which happens to be their side at.'

'Well, having gone there, what will Your Honour say?' asked

Rusty.

'Listen,' the other replied, 'in the first place I will find out if the master is pleased or displeased with me.'

'And what are the signs from which this can be discerned?' Rusty asked. Bossy said, 'Listen,

He looks towards you from afar;   (59, 60)
Smiles at you, and takes much care
In asking as to how you are;
And, even when you are not there,
Lauds your merits; and remembers
You among those he holds dear;
Your virtues from your faults dismembers;
And makes you gifts with words of cheer:
These are the signs which show the mind
Of the master being well inclined.

'Furthermore,

The signs discerning men should know,   (61)
Which the master's alienation show:
He encourages your hopes to grow,
But will not let them fructify
As in delays time passes by.

'Knowing all this, I will speak to him in such a way that he comes to rely on me. For,

The wise do show us vividly   (62)
How injudicious policy
In face of any quandary
Leads only to calamity,
While of proper means the use
A good conclusion will produce.'

'But you should not speak unless there is a suitable occasion,' said Rusty, 'for,

> Words out of turn, though even said (63)
> By a guru like Bṛhaspati,
> Would bring ridicule upon his head,
> And disgrace till eternity.'

'Do not be afraid, friend,' replied Bossy, 'I will not say anything unsuited to the occasion. For,

> When there is a wrong decision, (64)
> Or a critical, grave situation,
> Or when the time is passing on
> For something needing to be done—
> Though unasked, the servant must
> Speak out, faithful to his trust.

'If I do not give advice even when the occasion demands it, then I am not fit to be a minister. For,

> A virtue decent men admire, (65)
> Which also gives a livelihood,
> Should be raised to levels higher,
> And always guarded, well and good.

'Therefore, good sir, permit me. I am going.'

'Very well,' said Rusty, 'I wish you godspeed. Do as you will.'

Bossy, looking as if he was greatly disconcerted, then approached Tawny. Received politely by the king, he saluted him with an eightfold obeisance, and sat down at a distance.

'I am seeing you after a long time,' said the king.

'Although Your Majesty has little need for this servant,' replied Bossy, 'I have come nevertheless as it is essential for a vassal to present himself when the occasion calls for it. What is more,

The tooth to pick, the ear to scratch—   (66)
Even humble twigs can match
Some need of kings; then how much more
Can't those with speech and action sure.

'I have been disregarded since long, and even though Your
Majesty may suspect that I have lost my wits, yet there is
no need for any such doubt. For,

Though at one's foot the gemstone stay,   (67)
And on one's crown the piece of glass,
Even so, be that as it may,
A gem's a gem and glass is glass.

'Further,

Though a steadfast man is flouted,   (68)
His having wits should not be doubted.
The fire one may overturn:
Its flame will never downwards burn.

'Sire, a master must therefore be discriminating in every
way. For,

When the king lacks discrimination,   (69)
Treating all without distinction,
The ardour then will duly wane
Of those who best his work sustain.

'What is more,

Of men, O King, three types there are: (70)
The best, the worst, those on a par.
And so should they appointed be
To tasks of these categories three.

'For,

> Servants, as with jewellery,   (71)
> Should be kept in proper place.
> Diadems can't on ankles be,
> Nor anklets will the forehead grace.

'Besides,

> Gems worthy to be set in gold,   (72)
> If they are mounted on mere lead,
> They weep not, nor their gleam withhold:
> The setter is decried instead.

'Besides,

> A piece of glass placed in a crown,   (73)
> And gems in rings meant for the toe—
> Of gems therein no fault is known,
> 'Tis jewellers who thus their folly show.

'Look,

> The king who can their ways surmise,   (74)
> From servants has fulfillment clear:
> For one is loyal, brave or wise,
> And one there may be cause to fear.

'Similarly,

> The lute, the sabre, and the steed,   (75)
> Eloquence, law, mankind indeed,
> Depending in whose hands they be,
> Are good or bad, accordingly.

'Further,

Of what use is a devotee   (76)
Who has no capability?
Or someone who is able, true,
But bent always on harming you?
O King! I am both loyal and able,
And should not be thought despicable.

'For,

When kings their servants humiliate,   (77)
Only fools with them will stay.
When fools the councils dominate,
The wise will always keep away.
The state, abandoned by the wise,
Is meritless in policy.
And when it thus in tatters lies,
The people suffer misery.

'Furthermore,

A person whom the king venerates,   (78)
The people always eulogize.
But one the monarch denigrates,
They too will certainly despise.

'What is more,

A child's word even, if apposite,   (79)
Wise men should make use of it.
Don't we use the candle's light
When the sun has set at night?'

'My good Bossy,' said Tawny, 'What is this? You are the
son of our Prime Minister. But you have not come here for
such a long time because of what some villain may have
said. Now, say what you have on your mind.'

'Sire,' replied Bossy, 'I wish to ask something. Please tell me. The master is thirsty, but why then does he stand here looking so perplexed without drinking water?'

Tawny replied: 'You have spoken well. There was no one worthy of trust to whom I could talk about this secret. But you are trustworthy and so I will tell you. Listen. This forest now harbours some unknown being, and so we must abandon it. That is why I am perplexed. You too must have heard that great, unprecedented sound. Correspondingly, that creature must also be extremely strong.'

'Sire, this is indeed a cause for great concern,' said Bossy. 'We too have heard that sound. But which minister will first advise the abandonment of the land and afterwards a battle? In doubts concerning such matters, the utility of servants should be taken into account. For,

The worth of prowess and of mind   (80)
Of servants, spouse and family,
And himself too, will each man find
On the touchstone of calamity.'

'Good sir,' said the lion, 'a great fear has gripped me.'

'Otherwise why would you speak to me about giving up the pleasures of kingship and going somewhere else,' Bossy said to himself. Overtly, he replied, 'Sire, while I live you have nothing to fear. But Rusty and the others should also be reassured as it is difficult to assemble people at a time when trouble must be faced.'

Bossy and Rusty were then entertained by the king with all the means at his disposal. Both departed after promising to counter any danger. On the way, Rusty said to Bossy, 'Comrade, how is it that you accepted this lavish hospitality, and promised to remove his fears, without knowing their causes and if they can be countered or not? For, without rendering a service one should never accept a reward from anyone, specially from a king. Look,

> In his goodwill there lies treasure, (81)
> In his effort, victory,
> And death abides in his displeasure:
> All-powerful indeed is he.

'Similarly,

> The king, though young, by no means can (82)
> Be dismissed as no more than man,
> Because a great divinity
> In living human form is he.'

Bossy smiled and said: 'Friend, be quiet. I know the cause of his fear. That was only a bull bellowing. Bulls are even our prey, what to say of the lion's.'

'If that is so,' said Rusty, 'then why did you not allay the master's fears there and then?'

'If the master's fear had been relieved straightaway,' replied Bossy, 'then how could we have obtained this fine hospitality? Furthermore,

> The master, by his servants, never (83)
> Should be rendered free of need.
> If the servant does that, ever,
> Like White Ears he will be indeed.'

'How did that happen?' asked Rusty. Bossy narrated

The Cat which became Superfluous

On the hill called Mount Arbuda in the northern country there lived a lion named Mahāvikrama or Mightyvalour. A certain mouse would nibble the fringes of his mane every day as he slept in his mountain cave. Incensed to see his mane being snipped, and unable to catch the mouse which would dive into its burrow, he thought,

'If the enemy is too small,   (84)
By valour to be had at all,
To slay him one should organize
A soldier of an equal size.'

Having considered this, he went to the village and, placing his trust in a cat named Dadhikarṇa or White Ears, he brought it carefully to his cave where he nurtured it on a diet of meat.

Thereafter, the mouse stopped coming out of its hole for fear of the cat, and the lion slept in peace with his mane intact. Whenever he heard the mouse, he would encourage the cat by giving it an extra-special diet of flesh.

The mouse was tormented by hunger pangs. It came out at last and was caught and killed by the cat. Never again did the lion hear the sounds of the mouse in the burrow. No more having any use for the cat, he also lost interest in feeding it. Deprived of food, White Ears became feeble and eventually perished.

~

'It is for this reason that I said that the master should never be made free of need,' concluded Bossy. He and Rusty then approached Lively. Rusty sat down grandly under a tree, while Bossy went up to Lively, and said: 'You bull! this is General Rusty who has been appointed by King Tawny to guard the forest. He commands you to come before him immediately, or get out of our forest. Otherwise the consequences will be bad for you. I cannot say what our master will ordain if he is angered.'

Lively was unfamiliar with local ways. He came forward

diffidently and saluted Rusty with an eightfold prostration.
As it has been said,

> Intelligence is greater than (85)
> Strength of body, as one can
> See, in its absence, in the fate
> Of elephants led in captive state:
> This the drums do seem to say
> As mahouts beat them on the way.

Lively asked timidly: 'General, please tell me what I ought
to do.'

'If you hope to stay here in this forest,' replied Rusty,
'You must go and make obeisance at the lotus feet of our
lord.'

'I will go,' said Lively, 'but please give me your parole
of safe conduct. For that let Your Honour offer me his right
hand.'

'Listen, you bull,' said Rusty, 'enough of this suspicion.
For,

> Krishna did not deign reply (86)
> To curses Ćedi's king let fly.[2]
> Lions roar at thunder's peal,
> Not when jackals start to squeal.

'Further,

> The storm does not uproot the grass (87)
> Softly bent to let it pass.
> On tall trees only does it blow:
> The great their might to equals show.'

The two then left Lively at a distance, and went up to
Tawny. The king looked at them respectfully as they saluted
him and sat down.

'Have you seen him?' asked the king.

'He has been seen, sire,' said Bossy, 'he is, as Your Majesty had guessed, indeed immense. He wishes to meet Your Majesty. But he is very powerful, and you should be on guard when you see him. As to the sound, that by itself is not to be feared. As it is said,

One need not fear a sound alone   (88)
When its cause is still unknown.
Knowing of a sound the cause,
The procuress did gain applause.'

'How did that happen?' asked the king. Bossy narrated

The Canny Procuress

There is a town called Brahmapura on the Śrī mountain. It was rumoured that on ogre named Ghaṇṭākarṇa lived in the region of the mountain peak. Once a thief, running away with a large bell, was killed and eaten by a tiger. The bell, which had dropped from his hands, was found by some monkeys who used to ring it all the time.

The townspeople saw that a man had been devoured, and heard the constant ringing of the bell. Saying that the ogre was angry, and rang the bell as he ate humans, they all fled from the town. But there was a procuress named Karālā, who speculated, 'This bell rings without any occasion. Is it being rung by monkeys?' After finding out for herself, she went before the king saying: 'Sire, I will take care of this Ghaṇṭākarṇa if some money can be disbursed.'

The king gave some money to the procuress. She prepared the ritual circle and, having made therein an elaborate display of worshipping Gaṇeśa and other deities, herself went into the forest, carrying fruit which monkeys love.

She spread out the fruit, and the monkeys fell upon them, abandoning the bell. The procuress took it and returned to the town where she was honoured by everyone.

~

'That is why I said that one should not be scared by just a sound,' remarked Bossy. After the jackal had concluded his story, Lively was conducted and presented to the king, and began to live there happily. One day the lion's brother, another lion named Stabdhakarṇa or Prick-Ears, came by on a visit. Tawny received him with due courtesy and, having seated him, started to go out to catch some game for his dinner. Lively then said, 'Sire, where are the remains of the deer which were killed today?'

'Bossy and Rusty would know,' said the king.

'Do you know if anything is left or not?' asked Lively. The lion reflected. 'There isn't,' he said.

'How could they have consumed so much meat?' asked Lively.

'It may have been eaten, or given away, or gone bad,' observed the king. 'This is what happens every day.'

'How can this be done without Your Majesty's knowledge?' cried Lively.

'Well,' said the king, 'It is being done without my knowledge.'

'This is not proper,' Lively then remarked. 'As it is said,

The master's work should not be done,   (89)
Even trivial, on one's own
Without informing him before;
Unless it be a crisis sore
Which needs immediate countering
In the interest of the king.

'Further,

"What's but a moment's loss", who says— (90)
His are very foolish ways.
And one who scorns the poor farthing
Will stay in poverty, O King.
The minister must be like a pot
Which little yields, but holds a lot.

That minister is the best, (91)
Who daily swells the treasure chest
Even with a single pie;[3]
For the king's life does not lie
In his breath, as one can see,
But rather in his treasury.

Man reaches not an honoured station (92)
Just because of clan tradition.
Even his own wife will spurn
Him, should he a pauper turn.
The others do not us concern.

'And these are the principal defects in governing,

In finance the evils are: (93)
Excesses in expenditure
And lack of proper inspection;
Injustices in tax collection;
Fraud, which is like robbery;
And a remote authority.

'For,

Of income, never taking measure, (94)
Quick in spending at his pleasure,
Man will but face penury,
Though rich as the god of wealth he be.'

'Listen, brother,' said Prick-Ears, 'these two, Bossy and Rusty, have for long been your servants in charge of the duties of war and peace. They should never be appointed in charge of finance. I will also tell you what little I have heard on the subject of making appointments.

Priests, or warriors, or your kin,   (95)
Should never be considered in
Appointments to the treasury.
Of these, the first category,
Even if the revenue
Has been realized full and true,
Do not yield it, even though
Tortures they may undergo.

The warrior, when appointed to   (96)
The treasury, waves his sword at you;
While kinsmen all the money seize,
Saying it is the family's.

An officer in service long   (97)
Turns brazen, although in the wrong;
He holds his master in disdain;
His actions nothing can restrain.

Holding office, if there's one   (98)
Appointed for past favours done,
He admits not his own mistakes,
But credit for his favours takes,
And plunders everyone.

If one is a minister made,   (99)
Who as a child with you had played,
Then long acquaintance, certainly,
Will make him act cavalierly,
From which he is bound to bring

Himself to think he is the king.

The wicked, who are patient too,　　　　　(100)
Can indeed cause calamity:
Śakatāra and Śakuni[4] do
Give instance of this, Majesty.

Wealth will always, in the end,　　　　　(101)
Man to obduracy bind.
This is what the seers contend:
Opulence perverts the mind.

Not collecting monies due,　　　　　(102)
Embezzlement of revenue,
Pliancy and disinterest,
Unmindfulness of what is best,
And love of fleshly pleasures, are
Faults which do ministers mar.

The king must stratagems devise　　　　　(103)
To get at revenue that lies
With his officers, and always
Scrutinize their working ways,
Granting honours and citations,
Or moving them to other stations.

In most cases the functionary　　　　　(104)
Like a blister tends to be:
From the top unless you squeeze,
What's inside it won't release.

Officers who have made a pile—　　　　　(105)
The king should press them all the while.
With just one wring you cannot get
Much water from a towel wet.

'One should know all this, and put it into practice depending on the occasion.'

'I agree,' said Tawny, 'but these two never do what I tell them.'

'That is wholly improper,' retorted Prick-Ears, 'for,

> Those who the monarch disobey, (106)
> Never to be spared are they,
> His own children though they be.
> Otherwise how will one see
> The difference between a king
> In portraits, and the real thing?

'Further,

> The dull ruin their reputation, (107)
> The ill-natured their friendly ties,
> Senseless men, the clan tradition,
> The greedy ones, fair dharma's prize,
> Those prone to vice, the fruit of learning,
> The miserly, their happiness,
> And kings with deputies undiscerning,
> Ruin their sovereignty, no less.

'And, specially,

> From bandits, officers, foreign foes, (108)
> From favourites who to him are close,
> And from his own cupidity,
> The king must guard his citizenry:
> Like a father he should be.

'So, brother, follow my advice always. I too have dealt with such affairs. This Lively is a vegetarian. Put him in charge of your treasury.'

Arrangements were made in accordance with Prick-Ears'

advice. Thence onwards Tawny and Lively stopped associating with the others and passed their time in great amity. Bossy and Rusty saw a slackening in the provision of food, even for retainers, and consulted one another. 'Friend,' Bossy said to Rusty, 'what should be done? This problem is our own creation. There is hardly any point in complaining about one's own mistakes. As it has been said:

"Svarṇa Rekhā I did touch"; (109)
The procuress herself got bound;
The hermit craved for gems too much:
On ourselves do our faults redound.'

'How did that happen?' asked Rusty. Bossy related

Our Faults redound on Us

The city of Kanćhanapura was ruled by a king named Vīra Vikrama. His magistrate was once taking a certain barber to the execution ground when an itinerant ascetic named Kandarpa Ketu, who was accompanied by another hermit, caught hold of the hem of his garment and cried out: 'He is not to be executed!'

'Why shouldn't he be executed?' asked the royal officers. 'Listen,' replied the ascetic, and he proceeded to recite the verse "Svarṇa Rekhā I did touch" . . . and the rest. 'How did that happen?' asked the officers.

'My name is Kandarpa Ketu,' the ascetic said, 'and I am the son of Jīmūta Ketu, the king of Simhala island. Once, when I was at a pleasure park, I heard from a seafaring trader that on every fourteenth day a wish-fulfilling tree appeared in the middle of the ocean. Beneath it was a bed sparkling with gems, on which was to be seen a maiden like the goddess Lakshmī herself, adorned with all kinds of ornaments and playing upon a lute.

'Taking the merchant sailor, I went there on a ship, and

saw the girl on the divan in the water, as had been described. Charmed by her loveliness, I dived in after her and found myself in a city of gold. There I saw her on the divan in a golden palace, with demi-goddesses in attendance. She too saw me from a distance, and sent a companion who spoke to me respectfully.

'On my asking the companion, she told me that this was the daughter of Kandarpa Keli, the paramount ruler of the demi-gods called Vidyādhara. Ratna Manjarī was her name. She had vowed that the man who reached the city of gold and saw her there with his own eyes would marry her, even if her father was not present. The companion assured me that this was the maiden's intention, and advised me to marry her by the rule of mutual consent.

'So I married her by the rite of mutual consent,[5] and stayed there, enjoying myself with her. Once, when we were alone, she told me, "Lord, everything here is for you to enjoy as you will. But this likeness of the demi-goddess named Svarṇa Rekhā you should never touch." My curiosity was aroused and afterwards I touched Svarṇa Rekhā with my hand. Though she was only an image, she struck me with her lotus-like foot and I fell down and found myself in my own country.

'Deeply distressed, I became a wandering ascetic. I roamed all over the land and at last came to this city. Here I slept at the house of a cowherd yesterday.

'The cowherd came home in the evening from his friend's tavern, and discovered his wife in surreptitious discussion with a procuress. He thrashed his spouse and went to sleep after tying her to a pillar. At midnight the procuress, who is married to this barber, came back to the cowherd's wife and told her, "That gentleman is burning with desire for you. He has been struck by Kāma's arrow, and looks like one about to die. Seeing him in that condition has so upset me that I have come to help you. I will bind myself in your place and stay here. You go and satisfy him; but come back quickly.'

'This was duly done. After his wife had left, the cowherd suddenly woke up and cried out, "Now why don't you go to your lover?" When the procuress kept silent, he became angry. Shouting, "Are you too proud even to give me a reply?" he picked up a knife and cut off her nose. After that he fell asleep again.

'In due course the cowherd's wife came back. "Well, what happened?" she asked the procuress. "Look at my face," the latter replied, "that will tell you what happened!" Afterwards, the cowherd's wife tied herself up as before, and the procuress retrieved her amputated nose and went home.

'In the morning, when this barber asked for his box of razors, his wife gave him only one blade. Annoyed at not getting the whole box, the barber threw the razor back into the house. At this his wife began to wail loudly, crying that he had cut off her nose though she had done no wrong, and took him to the magistrate.

'As for the cowherd's wife, on being questioned again by her husband, she retorted, "You wretch! Who can dare to disfigure a supremely chaste woman like myself? The eight guardian gods alone know the spotlessness of my conduct. For,

Sun and moon who shine on high,   (110)
Water, fire, earth and sky,
The night, the day, the twilights two,
The gods of death and dharma true:
Man's actions all to them are known,
And to the heart he calls his own.

So, if I am indeed the first among chaste women, and have never even thought of anyone else other than you, my husband, then let my face become whole. Now, look at my face!"

'The cowherd lit a lamp and looked at her visage. When he saw that her nose was intact, he fell at her feet, exclaiming that he was blessed to have such a supremely virtuous wife.

'Listen also to the story of this hermit here. He left his home and spent twelve years on the slopes of the Malaya mountain before he came to this city. Here he slept in a bawdy house. On the threshold of the madam's door there stood a wooden statue of a goblin with a fine gemstone on its head. The hermit was greedy, and having noticed the gem, he got up at night and attempted to take it out. But he was caught in the statue's arms, which were operated by strings. His loud screams woke up the madam, who declared, "I know you have come from the Malaya region. Now give up all the gems you have to this goblin, otherwise he will not let you go, he is such a villain." So he had to surrender all his treasure and, now that he has lost everything, he too has joined me.

'After hearing all these accounts, the officers asked the magistrate to give a judgement. The barber's wife had her head shaved, the cowherd's spouse was exiled, and the procuress punished with a fine. The hermit's possessions were restored to him. The barber returned to his home.'

~

'It is for this reason,' said Bossy 'that I recited the verse beginning "Svarṇa Rekhā I did touch . . ." This problem is of our own making. There is no point in feeling sorry about it.' He thought for a moment and added, 'Friend, just as the sudden amity between these two was my creation, so too must I bring about a split in their friendship. For,

Clever people demonstrate   (111)
Even lies as verities:
As painters, on a level slate,

Show peaks as well as declivities.

'Furthermore,

One who's never at a loss   (112)
Even in situations new,
Will the hardest hurdles cross,
As the wife with lovers two.'

'How did that happen?' asked Rusty. Bossy narrated

The Woman with Two Lovers

In Dvāravāti there lived a cowherd whose wife was a whore.
She used to sleep with the village police chief as well as
with his son. As it is said,

The fire can't be satisfied   (113)
With all the wood that there may be.
All rivers flowing side by side
Cannot ever fill the sea.
Death its thirst can never slake
Though every creature it may take.
And a woman, it is sure
Of menfolk she needs ever more.

'Further,

By gifts one cannot win their heart,   (114)
Nor by praise or honest pleas,
Or being helpful, strong or smart,
For girls are always hard to please.

'For,

A husband young and handsome, rich and   (115)
                                    famous too

Also good at making love, and full of merits true,
But women, as soon as they can,
Will leave him for another man—
The lover, though he may have virtues
                                    very few.

'Furthermore,

Though sleep she may on couches rare,   (116)
The woman's pleasure can't compare
With that she gets on a dusty floor,
Lying with her paramour.

'Once, when she was in bed with the police chief's son, the
chief also arrived for the very same purpose. Seeing him on
the way, she hid the son in a cupboard and proceeded to
make love with the father. Then her husband, the cowherd,
returned from his cattle-pen. The cowherdess told the police
chief, "Pick up your staff and rush outside as if you are
angry." As he did this, the cowherd entered the house and
asked his wife what the police chief was doing there. "He
is angry with his son for some reason," the wife replied,
"the boy was on the road, and came in here. I hid him in
the cupboard to protect him. The father searched for him
here but could not find him. That is why he went out looking
so annoyed." She then got the son out of the cupboard and
showed him to her husband. As it has been said:

Women do eat twice as much   (117)
As men, in scriptures it is said;
Their intelligence is four times such
As man can have inside his head;
Their industry is six times more,
And eightfold is their passion's score.

'That is why I spoke about new situations,' said Bossy. 'That

may be so,' said Rusty 'but how will it be possible to cause
a rift in the deep affection that has grown between Tawny
and Lively because of their temperaments?'

'Some method will have to be devised,' said Bossy, 'As
it is said,

By stratagem what can be done, (118)
By valour can't be ever won:
Just as with a golden chain
The crow did have the serpent slain.'

'How did that happen?' asked Rusty. Bossy narrated

The Cunning Crow

On a certain tree there lived a crow couple. Their young
used to be eaten up by a black serpent who lived in a hollow
in the same tree. When the hen-crow became pregnant again,
she said to the crow, 'Lord, let us leave this tree. As long
as that black snake is here we will never have a family.
For,

A wicked wife, a villain friend, (119)
A servant who is insolent,
And a snake inside one's tenement:
These lead but to a fatal end.'

'Don't be afraid, my dear,' the crow replied. 'I put up many
times with his criminal activity, but now I will not tolerate
it any more.'

'He is very strong,' said the hen-crow,' how will you
fight him?'

'Don't worry,' the crow said, 'for,

He is strong who has a mind, (120)
The foolish strong can never be.

The lion with his swagger blind
Was finished by a rabbit, see.'

'And how could that happen?' the hen-crow asked with a smile. The crow narrated

The Lion and the Rabbit

'On the Mandara mountain there was a lion named, Durdānta or Haughty. He spent all his time killing the other animals. Those that remained got together and petitioned him, "Lord of beasts, why do you kill so many animals at the same time? If it please Your Majesty, we will ourselves present an animal to you every day for your food."

'"If this is what you gentlemen want," said the lion, "then let it be so." From then on he confined himself to feeding on the one animal which would be offered to him.

'Once it was the turn of an old rabbit. He said to himself,

"To plead with slayers one could try,   (121)
For getting on one's life a lease;
But if I am now sure to die,
For what should I this lion please?

So I will take my time in going to him."

'The lion was meanwhile famished. "Why have you come so late?" he asked the rabbit angrily.

'"Sire, it is not my fault," said the rabbit. "I was on my way here, but on the road I was detained forcibly by another lion. I had to swear to return to him. Now I have come here to report this to Your Majesty."

'The lion was incensed. "Where is that villain?" he cried. "Go immediately and show that wretch to me!"

'The rabbit then took the lion to a deep well. There he showed him his own reflection in the water. "Master, see for yourself," he said. The enraged lion flung himself imperiously upon his own reflection and perished there and then.

~

'That is why I said that he alone is strong who has a mind,' the crow continued. 'I heard it all,' said his wife. 'Now tell me what is to be done.'

'A prince comes here every day to bathe in the nearby lake,' said the crow. 'At that time he takes off a golden chain that he wears, and keeps it on the stone steps leading to the water. Pick it up with your beak, and place it in this hollow.'

When the prince had got into the water, the hen-crow did as she had been told. The officers looking for the golden chain saw the black serpent inside the hollow of the tree, and killed it.

'That is why I spoke about what can be done by stratagems,' said Bossy. 'If that is so,' replied Rusty, 'then carry on, and may all go well with you.'

Bossy then went to Tawny and, after saluting him, said, 'Sire, I have come as I consider that there is an extremely dangerous emergency. For,

A true well wisher always ought   (122)
To give good counsel, though unsought:
When there is a wrong decision,[6]
Or a critical, grave situation,
Or when the time is passing on
For something needing to be done.

'Further,

Pleasure is a kingly perk: (123)
For ministers it should be work.
A minister who spoils the same,
From every side is held to blame.

'The proper course for ministers is this:

Life it's better to forsake, (124)
Even by decapitation,
Rather than no notice take
Of someone with the aspiration
—Though it is a dreadful sin—
To seize the post his master's in.'

'What do you want to say, sir?' Tawny enquired politely.
Bossy said: 'Sire, it looks as if Lively is adopting an improper
attitude towards you. Between us, he has disparaged the
triple powers[7] of Your Majesty, and covets this kingdom
itself.'

On hearing this Tawny was struck dumb with fear and
surprise. 'Sire,' continued Bossy, 'you removed all the other
ministers and made him alone in charge of everything. That
was the real mistake. For,

A minister if the king exalt (125)
Too much in strength, it is a fault.
For then the goddess Sovereignty
Resting on them both will be.
And such balance is hard to bear
For someone of the gender fair;
So, of the two, all said and done,
She surely will abandon one.

'Furthermore,

If one the king should elevate (126)

As chief minister of the state,
That will likely turn his head,
On vainglory he will be fed,
Pride will make him indolent,
And then will in his heart ferment
The desire for autonomy,
Prelude to acts of treachery,
Which may possibly extend
To putting the king's life to an end.

'Further,

For wheat which is infected,   (127)
A tooth which shakes when pressed,
And a minister disaffected,
Extirpation is the best.

'What is more,

A king who lets his sovereignty   (128)
With his counsellors reside,
Will, when he is in difficulty,
Be like the blind without a guide.

'And the minister then does everything just as he pleases. But you, master, are the authority here. As for me, I know this:

In this world there's not a man   (129)
Who does not crave authority;
Another's handsome wife who can
Not ogle at but wistfully.'

The lion reflected for a while. 'My good fellow,' he said, 'it may be as you say. But I still have a deep affection for Lively. Look,

Someone dear is someone dear (130)
Though he may act improperly.
One loves one's body, it is clear,
Even though sick it may be.

'Further,

Something dear is something dear, (131)
To harming one though it may turn.
One respects fire, it is clear,
Though one's house it cause to burn.'

Bossy said: 'Sire, this indeed is the mistake. For,

Of whoever the king makes more, (132)
Of his eyes the cynosure—
It may be his very son,
A minister or just anyone—
To that person's side will come
Sovereignty to seek a home.

'Listen, sire,

Unpleasant but good advice (133)
Has consequences always nice.
But it needs a giver and
One who will it understand.
Wherever both are found to be,
There flourishes all prosperity.

'You ignored your old servants and rewarded this newcomer.
That was not proper. For,

There is indeed no greater fault (134)
Disruptive of affairs of state,
Than the new men to exalt

And servants old repudiate.'

'This is most surprising,' said the lion. 'How can he betray
me when I brought him here with a promise of safe conduct
and looked after him?'

'Sire,' replied Bossy,

The wicked, though helped night and day,   (135)
True to their own nature stay.
Though it may be sweated hard
And straightened out with some pomade,
All this is of no avail
For a curling canine tail.

'Furthermore,

Massaged hard to make it sweat,   (136)
Circumscribed inside a net,
Kept thus a dozen years or more:
The dog's tail still is as before.

'Further,

Can honours and promotions please   (137)
The wicked? They're like poison trees,
Which watered with pure nectar though,
Will never fruit nutritious grow.

'That is why I say,

If you do not wish to see   (138)
Someone in adversity,
Even though he may not ask it,
Tell him what is for his benefit.
That's the truly virtuous way—

Anything else, a wicked play.

'And, as it has been said,

> That person really loves you well,   (139)
> Who helps you out of evil's spell.
> A real friend indeed is he,
> Who has no insincerity.
> The person who has wisdom sure
> Is one all good people will adore.
> That's real action, which is true;
> And that a wife, who follows you.
> That is true prosperity,
> Which does not lead to vainglory.
> He is happy deemed to be,
> Who has become from cravings free;
> And he a real man and whole,
> Who keeps his urges in control.

'The king is under threat from Lively. If he does not take care, even after being warned, it should not be considered this servant's fault. For,

> When the king, intent on pleasure,   (140)
> Of his duties loses measure,
> And of his true interest, but
> Like an elephant mad with rut,
> Goes heedless wherever he will,
> Filled with pride and arrogance, till
> He falls into a pit of woe:
> Then he blames his servants, though
> He still cannot at all realize—
> The fault in his own conduct lies.'

Tawny said to himself:

'Others one should not condemn (141)
On someone else's accusation,
But reward or punish them
After one's own investigation.

'For it is said,

Without a due determination (142)
Of fault or merit, one should not
Give punishment or approbation—
One's own ruin thus is sought,
Like if you put your hand inside
A serpent's mouth, just out of pride.

'Should I then dismiss Lively?' he asked Bossy. 'Not at all,
sire,' the latter replied quickly, 'in that way your consultations
will get compromised. As it is said,

The seed of consultation (143)
Always keep concealed:
It has no germination
If even slightly revealed.

'What is more,

If taking, giving, as is due, (144)
Or other work which should be done,
Is not attended swiftly to
In time, its essence then is gone.

'As such it is essential that every effort should be made to
complete without delay whatever has been started. For,

Though guarded well in every way, (145)
A regiment feeling insecure
Will not long in one place stay

For fear that enemies will procure
An opening: it is the same
With consultations in all but name.

'It would be extremely imprudent to try to change his ways
by placating him, when he has already committed treason.
For,

One who seeks to reinstate   (146)
A friend who has him once betrayed—
Sure disaster is his fate:
It's like a she-mule pregnant[8] made.'

'Not knowing the proper state   (147)
Of how the big and small relate,
How can one take a view
On what a person cannot do?
Look, how the ocean was deterred
By the lapwing, such a little bird.'

'How did that happen?' the lion asked. Bossy narrated

The Lapwing and the Ocean

A lapwing couple lived on the shore of the southern ocean.
When it was time for the mother bird to lay her eggs, she
told her mate, 'Lord, please look for a secluded place suitable
for my labour.'

'Wife,' said the lapwing, 'surely this place itself is suitable
for your confinement.'

'But this place gets flooded when the tide comes in,' she
replied.

'What!' cried the lapwing, 'am I so powerless that the
ocean should insult me inside my own house?'

'My lord,' the mother bird said with a smile, 'there is a
great difference between you and the ocean. Or, rather,

It is hard oneself to know   (148)
If one is able, or not so.
If such discrimination there could be,
One would not suffer misery.

'Besides,

Starting something unworthy,   (149)
Enmity with your own kin,
With the powerful, rivalry,
And giving credence to women:
It is said that all these four
To self-destruction are the door.'

Nevertheless she was persuaded, though with some difficulty, by her husband's words and went into labour there itself. Meanwhile the ocean had overheard all their conversation. In order to test how strong they were, it carried away all their eggs.

The mother bird was besides herself with grief. 'Lord,' she cried to her mate, 'it is a disaster! My eggs are gone!'

'Do not be afraid, my dear,' said the lapwing. He held a meeting with the other birds and then went to Garuḍa, who is the lord of all the denizens of the air. There he recounted the entire episode and appealed to the celestial eagle, 'Sire, I have been humiliated by the ocean inside my own house though I had done nothing wrong.'

After hearing the lapwing's petition, the divine Garuḍa submitted it to his master, the god Nārāyaṇa, who is the creator, the preserver and the destroyer of this universe. The god ordered the ocean to return the eggs and, in reverent compliance with the divine commandment, it handed them over to the lapwing.

~

'That is why I talked about knowing the relationship between the small and the great,' concluded Bossy.

'How can it be ascertained if Lively has treason on his mind?' asked the king.

'When he comes arrogantly, his horns ready to lunge as if in confusion, it is then that Your Majesty will know.' Saying this, Bossy got up and went to Lively. Approaching him slowly, he pretended to be in a state of uncertainty.

'Good sir,' Lively asked politely, 'is all well with you?' 'How can all be well with servants?' said Bossy. 'For,

State servants are so insecure, (150)
Their goods the king can always seize.
Of their lives they can't be sure:
Their minds can never be at ease.

'Further,

Who, on attaining affluence, (151)
Does not succumb to arrogance?
When given up to pleasures, who
Can to trouble bid adieu?
Who has never jilted been
By women on this earthly scene?
Who escapes death's fearful sting?
And who's the favourite of the king?
Which beggar ever gets respect?
Which man is there who can expect,
When fallen in a villain's snare,
To come out safe, without a care?'

'Tell me comrade,' asked Lively, 'what is the matter?' 'What can I say,' Bossy replied, 'it's my misfortune. Look,

What now to do, I do not know— (152)
Just like the man who can't let go

> Or hold on to the deadly snake
> He grabs, when drowning in a lake.

'For,

> Here the royal trust will end, (153)
> There perishes a trusting friend.
> I'm plunged into a sea of woe.
> What can I do? Where can I go?'

Saying this, Bossy sighed deeply and sat down. 'Even so, friend,' Lively persisted, 'do tell me clearly what is in your heart.'

Bossy said with a furtive air, 'Even though what the king says in confidence is not to be spoken about, you came here trusting in me and I do not want to spoil the chance of my going to heaven. So I must tell you what is in your interest. Listen. This king has turned against you. He has said privately that he is going to kill you to please his family.'

Lively was deeply distressed. 'Stop looking so dejected,' Bossy continued, 'you must act while there is still time.' Lively thought for a while, and observed, 'It is indeed well said,

> In most cases it is so: (154)
> Women will to villains go;
> Kings prefer to patronize
> Those who least deserve to rise;
> Wealth waits upon the miserly;
> And on mountains, or the sea,
> Do the heavens shower rain
> (Rather than on fertile plain.)

'Is it this jackal's doing,' he wondered, 'or is it not? It is not possible to discern this from his behaviour. For,

From his master's majesty   (155)
A villain, too, draws dignity.
The lustre of a damsel's eyes
Her dark mascara glorifies.

'What a mess this is. For,

One tries to propitiate a king;   (156)
If he's not pleased, it's no strange thing.
But this was never known to be:
Well served, he turns an enemy.'

'It is impossible to fathom this. For,

Someone who has indicated   (157)
For his anger specific cause,
Can for certain be placated
By correcting what it was.
But one who harbours in his mind
Some groundless animosities:
How can any person find
A way for such a one to please?

'How have I harmed the king?' he then asked. 'Or, is it
that kings can turn hostile for no reason at all?'
    'It is indeed like that,' said Bossy. 'Listen,

Even though a helpful turn   (158)
Is by wise well-wishers done,
It can hostility earn,
While others may have favour won
Though doing actual injury.
For royal minds are hard to know—
They are not prone to constancy.
Even yogis think it so—
A servant it is hard to be.

'Further,

> A hundred favours to them done, (159)
> For the wicked, are as none.
> A hundred verses will go waste
> On those without artistic taste.
> A hundred times though one may plead,
> It's lost on those who pay no heed.
> And good advice, a hundredfold,
> On the mindless has no hold.

'What is more,

> Fragrant is the sandal tree, (160)
> But on it snakes are also found.
> In water there may lilies be,
> But also crocodiles abound.
> And in pleasure there always are
> Villains who its merits mar.
> One cannot have felicity
> Entirely of problems free.

'Further,

> In its roots are serpents found, (161)
> On its flowers bees abound,
> On branches monkeys shelter take,
> A home above the wild bears make.
> There's nothing of a sandal tree,
> Sweetly fragrant though it be,
> On which there does not always feature
> Some wicked or some violent creature.

'As for this master of ours, I know that he talks sweetly,
but he has a poisonous heart. For,

Wherefrom have the wicked learnt   (162)
Such drama, never seen before—
The hand, in greeting, upward turned,
The eyes which well with teardrops pure.
On his own seat he offers place,
And displays every consideration.
He's ready with a close embrace
And much pleasing conversation.
But he is a master of deceit:
Poison hidden in a sweet.

'Similarly,

A ship, to cross the fearful seas,   (163)
A lamp, the darkness to dispel,
A fan, for when there is no breeze,
A goad, to guide the elephant well—
Thus there is nothing in creation
For which a cure has not been thought,
Except the villainous inclination,
Cure which even God cannot.'

Lively sighed again. 'What a mess!' he cried. 'Why should
I, a mere herbivore, deserve execution by the lion? For,

A dispute one can understand   (164)
Between those whose riches and
Whose power is of equal station.
But between the very great
And those who are of lowest state,
It is beyond all explanation.

'I do not know who could have turned this king against
me,' Lively thought again. 'But a king who has become
unfriendly is something always to be feared. For,

The monarch's thinking, if it may (165)
From the minister turn away,
Who can ever bring it back?
It's like a crystal with a crack.

'Further,

The lightning and the monarch's ire, (166)
Terror do they both inspire.
The first, though, strikes at just one place,
The latter, from all sides you face.

'So, one should fight, even till death. For now it is no longer
worthwhile to obey his orders. For,

Slain, one will to heaven go, (167)
Or happy be by slaying the foe.
Either goal is hard to gain,
But one, the valiant can attain.

'And this is the time for engaging in battle,

(168)

When fighting one alive may stay,
But not to fight will make death sure,
Then, as all the sages say,
It is indeed the time for war.

'For,

When, without recourse to war, (169)
No benefit does the wise man see,
He goes to battle, ready for
Death besides the enemy.

Wealth one has in victory, (170)
In death the joys of paradise.

> This body is but transitory—
> Why fret if it in battle dies?'

Having reflected over all this, Lively said, 'O friend, how will I know that the lion is intent on killing me?'

Bossy replied. 'When he glares at you with his tail erect, his paws upraised, and his jaws wide open, then you too should display your mettle. For,

> Even the strong, when lacking spirit,   (171)
> Are thought no better than the dead.
> Look at that ash heap, no spark in it—
> How fearlessly men on it tread.

'But all this must be kept very secret. Otherwise both you and I will be finished.' And, with these words, Bossy returned to Rusty.

'Well?' asked Rusty. 'Is it done?'

'It is done,' Bossy replied, 'a split between the two of them has been accomplished.'

'Was there any doubt!' Rusty cried, 'for,

> For villains, who is ever a friend?   (172)
> Who has no skills in mischief got?
> Whose joy in wealth can ever end?
> And, importuned, who angers not?

'Further,

> The wicked, for their personal gain,   (173)
> Will lead the virtuous into vice.
> Their company is a real bane,
> It harms, like fire, in a trice.'

Then Bossy went back to Tawny. 'Sire, that traitor is here! Get ready and be on guard!' Saying this he got the lion to assume the posture he had earlier described to the bull. Lively had arrived meanwhile, and, seeing the lion in such a terribly transformed state, he too went through his own paces. In the great battle which then ensued between them, Lively was killed by the lion.

Having slain Lively, the lion stood at rest, looking sad. 'What a terrible deed have I done!' he said, 'For,

> While others enjoy his own estates, (174)
> The king himself has sin incurred,
> When dharma's limits he violates,
> Like the lion who killed the elephant herd.

'Furthermore,

> As between their losing hold (175)
> Of a part of territory,
> And a servant, wise and old,
> The latter death for kings can be.
> For lost land's easier to regain
> Than good servants to get again.'

'What is this new logic, Master,' said Bossy, 'that you feel so sorry after having eliminated an enemy? As it is said,

> If the king does truly care (176)
> For his interests and welfare,
> Should his own father, or his son,
> His brother, or an intimate friend,
> His life threaten, he for one
> Should quickly put theirs to an end.

'Besides,

> One who the essence comprehends (177)
> Of the triple human ends[9]

Should not have excessive pity.
The too forgiving lose ability
To safeguard even what they hold
In their hands, of grain or gold.

'What is more,

Forgiveness to friend or foe,   (178)
For monks may be an excellence.
But kings, if it will also show
To criminals—it then makes no sense.

'Furthermore,

One who seeks his master's throne   (179)
For ego's sake, or greedy grown—
The only way to make amends
For him is that his life he ends.

'Further,

A king too tender on the whole,   (180)
A priest given to gluttony,
A wife resistant to control,
An ally prone to villainy,
An officer with a careless way,
A servant who will not obey,
And men who have no gratitude:
All these need to be eschewed.

'And specially,

Sometimes false, at others true,   (181)
Harsh, and sweetly-worded too,
Both kind and cruel the king must be,
Magnanimous and miserly,

Given to much lavish spending,
But with taxation never ending.
Like a harlot, kingly ways
Must many faces wear always.'

Thus reassured by Bossy, Tawny sat upon his throne with
his natural spirits regained. And Bossy, gleefully proclaiming
'Victory to the great king! May all be well with everyone!'
lived happily as before.

'*Y*our Highnesses,' concluded Viṣṇu Śarma, 'you have now
learnt the methods of Splitting of Partners.' 'We learnt it by
Your Honour's grace,' said the princes, 'we are very pleased.'
'May there be this also,' said Viṣṇu Śarma:

'May Splitting of Partners only be   (182)
In the camps of your adversary.
May the wicked go a fatal way,
And meet destruction every day.
May joy and all prosperity
Among the people always be;
And may children ever play
In this grove of stories gay.'

Vigraha

War

*I*t was time to resume the discourse. 'We are princes, Noble Sir,' said the princes, 'and we are curious to learn about war.' 'I will speak on whatever interests Your Highnesses,' Viṣṇu Śarma replied, 'listen to *Vigraha* or War, of which this is the first stanza:

> In the late war which took place   (1)
> Between the swan and peacock race,
> Equal prowess both displayed,
> But swans were by the crows betrayed,
> Who won their trust while they did dwell
> Inside the enemy's citadel.'

'How did that happen?' asked the princes. Viṣṇu Śarma narrated the following story:

*I*n the island of Karpūra there is a lake called Padmakeli. By it there lived a swan of the royal breed named Hiraṇyagarbha or Goldegg. All the water birds had got together and anointed him as their king. For,

> If there be no king to lead   (2)
> The populace, it sinks indeed
> Like a ship with unmanned helm
> Launched upon the sea-god's realm.

Furthermore,

The king protects the populace,   (3)
They bring to him prosperity.
But protecting must have pride of place—
Without it there would nothing be.

Once the swan king was sitting at ease on a lotus bed,
surrounded by his courtiers, when a crane named
Dīrghamukha or Bigmouth arrived from somewhere and took
a seat after making his salutations.

'Bigmouth,' said the king, 'you have come from foreign
lands. Give us all the news.'

'Sire, there is some important news,' the crane replied,
'it is to inform you that I have rushed here. Listen. On
Jambu island there is a hill called Vindhya. A king of the
birds, a peacock by the name of Citravarṇa or Dapple, lives
there. His servants saw me in the Dagdharaṇya forest while
I was passing through. "Who are you?" they asked me,
"from where have you come?" I told them that I was a
servant of the royal swan Goldegg, the sovereign lord of
Karpūra island, and that I had come there out of curiosity
to see foreign lands.

'After listening to me those birds asked, "Which is the
better one among our two countries and kings?" "What a
question!' said I, 'there is no comparison. Karpūra island is
like heaven itself, and our swan king is a second lord of
paradise. What are you all doing stuck in this desert? Come,
let us go to my country."

'On hearing my words they all became angry. As it is
said,

When serpents on good milk are fed,   (4)
It only makes their venom grow.
Fools, with words of counsel said,
Are never pleased, but anger show.

'Further,

Give counsel only to the wise,   (5)
Never to the ignorant.
The birds to monkeys gave advice,
And had to leave their tenement.'

'How did that happen?' asked the king. Bigmouth narrated

The Birds who tried to help the Monkeys

There is a giant silk-cotton tree at the foot of a hill by the side of the river Narmadā. Many birds had built nests in it and lived there happily, even when it rained. Once, during the monsoon season, the sky was covered with banks of clouds like dark blue mantles, and it rained incessantly. Some monkeys crowded under the tree, shivering in the cold. The birds were moved by pity on seeing them. They said, 'Listen, O you monkeys,

We built nests with bits of straw,   (6)
Which with our beaks alone we brought.
Why do you such pain endure,
When hands and feet you all have got?'

The monkeys were enraged. 'These birds!' they said to themselves, 'sitting comfortably inside their nests protected from the blast, they dare to criticize us? Well, just let it stop raining.' And once the shower had ceased, they climbed up the tree, destroyed all the nests, and threw down the eggs from inside them.

~

'That is why I said that counsel should only be given to the wise,' said the crane. 'What did they do then?' the king asked.

The crane said: 'Those birds were enraged. "Whoever made that swan a king?" they exclaimed. I too was incensed. "And whoever made your peacock a king?" I retorted. On hearing this they were ready to kill me. I also got ready to fight. For,

> At other times it does behoove (7)
> For menfolk to forbearing be,
> And for maidens so to move
> As befits their modesty.
> Except in combat and in love,
> Brave should one, and bold the other, prove.'

The king smiled and said,

> 'One who having analysed (8)
> His own and others' abilities,
> The difference has not still realized,
> Is scorned by all his enemies.

'Further,

> Within a tiger's skin concealed, (9)
> A foolish ass for long did graze
> Daily in the farmer's field
> Till he was killed by his own brays.'

'How did that happen?' the crane asked. The king narrated

The Ass Disguised as a Tiger

In the town of Hastināpura there was a washerman named Vilāsa. His ass had been so worn out by carrying burdens that it seemed to be on the point of death. The washerman covered the ass with a tiger skin and put it out to graze in a field of corn near a forest. The farmers used to see it from a distance and run away quickly, thinking that it was a tiger.

One of the guards looking after the corn once took up a position in a quiet place. He had protected his body with a grey blanket and crouched low with his bow and arrow held ready. Seeing him from afar, the ass, who had grown stout and strong eating the corn at leisure, concluded that the other animal was a female donkey. It rushed forward, braying loudly. Its screams made it clear to the guard that this was only an ass, and he killed it in a trice.

~

'That is why I mentioned the ass in the field,' said the swan king. 'Well, what happened then?'

'Then,' continued Bigmouth, 'Those birds exclaimed, "You villain! You wretched crane! You walk about our land, and abuse our master! This cannot be tolerated any more." And all of them began to peck at me with their beaks, shouting angrily, "You fool! Just look at that swan, your king! He is too mild and not fit to rule at all. For, one who is mild cannot protect even that which he has in the palm of his hand. How can he rule on earth? What does a kingdom mean to him? And you are no better than a frog in a well for preaching shelter with him. Listen,

> For shelter seek a noble tree, (10)
> Shady, and with fruit arrayed.
> If fruit, by chance, there should not be,
> Still, who can take away the shade?

"Further,

> Even milk if barmaids carry, (11)
> Wine by others 'twill be thought.

So with the base one should not tarry—
Let company of the great be sought.

"Further,

Merits, though of great extent,   (12)
Shrink in contact with the mean,
As with the lordly elephant,
When in a little mirror seen.
The image which the glass portrays
Depends on how big is its base.

"And specially,

When a king is truly great,   (13)
On his name will success wait,
Though mentioned only in pretence;
As was the happy consequence
For the rabbits who did use
The moon god's title as a ruse."

"'How did that happen?'" I asked. The birds narrated

The Rabbit and the Elephant

Once there was no rain, even during the monsoon season. A herd of elephants was beside itself with thirst. 'Lord,' the elephants said to the leader of the herd, 'how are we going to live? Only small animals can use the water here and we, who are unable to do so for lack of space, are almost going blind. Where can we go, and what should we do?'

The leader of the herd then went some distance and showed the other elephants a lake full of clear water. Little rabbits lived on its banks and, as the days passed, they started getting hurt and crushed under the elephants' feet.

A rabbit named Śilīmukha or Dartface began to worry.

'These thirsty elephants are bound to come here every day.
Our entire tribe will then be destroyed.' But an aged rabbit
called Vijaya or Victor declared, 'Do not be despondent. I
will solve this problem.' And he went away after making
this vow.

'How can I stand before a herd of elephants and speak?'
Victor said to himself as he went,

'By touch itself can elephants kill;   (14)
By sniffs alone the serpents will;
Sovereigns with a smile do slay;
And villains as they homage pay.

'So I will climb on top of a hill and then address the leader
of the herd.'

After Victor had thus positioned himself, the leader of
the herd asked him, 'Who are you? From where have you
come?'

'I am a rabbit,' said Victor, 'I have been sent, sir, by the
moon god to you.'

'State your business,' said the herd leader. Victor said,

'The envoy does not speak a lie,   (15)
Though weapons may be raised on high.
Always deemed inviolate,
The truth for certain he will state.

'Therefore I will speak as I have been commanded. Listen.
This is the lake of the moon, and these rabbits are its
guardians. You have acted improperly in displacing them,
for they have been under my protection for a long time. It
is for that reason that I, the moon, am well known for
having the rabbit[1] as my emblem.'

Thus addressed by an envoy, the leader of the elephants
said defensively, 'We acted out of ignorance. We will not
come here again.' The envoy told him, 'If that is so, then

salute the moon god to seek his grace, and go. He is in the lake, trembling with anger.'

That night the rabbit took the leader of the herd to the lake, showed him the moon's reflection shimmering in the water, and made him salute it. 'O god,' he intoned, 'they committed this sin out of ignorance. Please forgive them. They will not repeat it again.' And with these words, the elephants were sent away.

~

'It is for this reason that I said that success waits upon a king's name and fame,' the crane continued. 'Then I told those birds, "Our lord the swan king is very mighty and exceedingly potent. He could be the master of all the three worlds, what to say of a mere kingdom." At this the birds again berated me, "Wretch! How dare you come into our territory!" Then they took me to king Dapple.

'They presented me before the king and, after saluting him, said, "Your attention, sire! This wretched crane has been abusing Your Majesty even while wandering about our country."'

'"Who is he?" asked the king. "From where has he come?" The birds replied, "He has come from Karpūra island. He is a servant of the royal swan Goldegg." The minister, a vulture, asked me, "Who is the Prime Minister there?" "The goose Sarvajña or Knowall," I replied. "He is an expert in all the sciences." "That is good," said the vulture, "he is from the king's own country. For,

Hailing from the king's own land,   (16, 17)
Nobly bred, immaculate, and
Of tried and proven honesty,
Good counsellor, of vices free,
Who won't from rightness deviate,

Whose ancestors have served the state,
Adept in matters of dispute,
Learned, and of high repute;
Finally, a person who
Excels in raising revenue—
To such a one, the sovereign should
Give, properly, ministerhood."

'Then a parrot spoke up, "Sire, Karpūra and other minor islands are a part of Jambu island itself. They are also under Your Majesty's sovereignty." "That is so," the king replied, "For,

What need is there to speak again   (18)
Of things it's possible to attain,
When only what they cannot get
Is the thing that kings covet?
Of children this is also true,
And of pretty maidens too,
As of those whom wealth makes vain,
Or those who have become insane."

'To this I responded, "If sovereignty flows from mere words, then the island of Jambu too is in the dominion of our lord Goldegg." "And how will this be decided?" cried the parrot. "By war alone!" said I. "Then go and get your master ready," the king observed with a smile.

'I then told the king: "You should also send your ambassador with me." "Who will go as the ambassador?" the king said, "for, to appoint one,

An ambassador must always be   (19)
Loyal, marked by purity,
Of proper merit, skilled, mature,
With a ready wit and sure,
Free from vice of any kind,

Quick to read another's mind,
And a cleric[2] he should be—
Such is the ideal emissary."

'"There are many who can be ambassadors,' said the vulture,
"but only one of the priestly caste should be appointed. For,

His master he will always please,   (20)
And never covet his properties.
His nature, like the inky shade
Of poison, even Śiva cannot fade.[3]"

'"Then let the parrot go," said the king. "Parrot, go with
this bird and speak on my behalf." "As you command, sire,"
the parrot replied, "but this crane is a villain. So I will not
go with him. As it is said,

A criminal act the wicked do,   (21)
Its fruit upon the good redound.
Rāvana kidnapped Sitā, true—
But it was Ocean who was bound.

"Furthermore,

With villains one should never go   (22)
Nor stay, as witness with the crow
The swan who stayed, the quail who went:
Both met a fatal accident."

'"How did that happen?" the king asked. The parrot
narrated

The Swan and the Crow

"There is a giant fig tree by the side of the road to Ujjayinī,
on which there lived a swan and a crow. Once in the summer

a tired traveller had gone to sleep under the tree, a bow and arrow by his side. After some time the tree's shade moved away from his face, exposing it to the fierce sunlight. The swan, which sat on the tree, was moved to pity on seeing this, and spread his wings to shade the traveller's face once more. Sleeping soundly, the traveller yawned with pleasure. But the crow, who was villainous by nature, was unable to tolerate the comfort of others. So he emptied his bowels into the traveller's open mouth and flew away. When the latter jumped up and looked above, all he could see was the swan, whom he shot with his arrow and killed forthwith.

"That is why I said that one should never stay with villains. Now I will tell you the story of

The Crow and the Quail

*O*nce all the birds proceeded to the sea-shore in connection with a pilgrimage by their lord Garuḍa. On that occasion the quail went with the crow. As they travelled, the crow repeatedly stole and ate curds from the pot which a cowherd was carrying on his head. When the cowherd put down his pot of curds and looked up, he saw both the crow and the quail above. The crow flew swiftly and got away, but the slow-moving quail was caught and killed by the cowherd. That is why I said that one should neither stay nor go with villains."

~

'Then,' continued the crane, 'I protested, "Brother Parrot, why do you speak like this? For me Your Honour is no less than His Majesty."

'"That may be so," the parrot replied, "but,

Whatever the wicked say,   (23)
Smiling sweetly be it may,
For perturbation does give reason,
Like flowers blooming out of season.

"As for wickedness, that is quite clear from Your Honour's own words. They alone are causing this confrontation between our two kings. Look,

Though harm is done before their eyes,   (24)
Sweet talk the foolish satisfies.
The chariot-maker did adore
His own wife bedding a paramour."

'The king asked, "How did that happen?" The parrot narrated

The Fool who was Easily Satisfied

'There was a chariot-maker named Mandamati who lived in the city of Yauvanaśrī. He knew that his wife was having an affair, but had never seen her together with her lover with his own eyes. So he went out one day, saying that he was going to another village. But, having gone some distance, he returned home secretly and hid himself under the bed.

Believing that the chariot-maker had indeed gone to another village, his wife invited her lover to come that very evening. As they were making passionate love on the bed, a sudden movement made her aware that her husband was underneath. This disconcerted her somewhat, whereupon her lover asked, 'What is the matter? Today your embraces are not as ardent as usual. You seem distracted.'

'You do not understand,' she said. 'He, who is the lord of my life, and my comrade since I was a girl, has gone to another village today. Without him this place seems to me like a wilderness, even though it is full of so many people.

What will happen to him in strange surroundings, what will he eat, and where will he sleep, are questions which stab at my heart.'

'What!' said the lover, 'is your chariot-maker so dear to you?' 'You barbarian,' the adulteress retorted, 'how dare you say this! Listen,

Even though he harshly speak, (25)
And glare at her most angrily,
The virtuous wife will always seek,
Happy with her lord to be.

'Furthermore,

The husband may in cities stay, (26)
Or in forests far away,
Sinful in his conduct be,
Or lead a life of purity—
The wife who loves him even so,
To paradise is bound to go.

'Further,

Of all the others they may wear, (27)
There can be no ornament
For womankind more excellent
Than to have the husband near.
Without him they cannot shine,
Glittering though with jewellery fine.

'You are a lover, who serves as a diversion once in a while, like a flower or a betel leaf. He is my master, who may sell me or give me away to the gods or even to the brahmins. What more is there to say? I live while he lives, and when he dies I have decided to follow him in death also. For,

More than thirty million be (28)
The hair upon this human frame—
That many years lives blissfully
In paradise the noble dame
Who follows still, when he is dead,
The lord and husband she had wed.

'Further,

As from its pit the lurking snake (29)
The catcher draws out forcibly,
So does she her husband take
To heaven, and there blessed be.

'Furthermore,

The wife who mounts his funeral pyre, (30)
Embracing her husband late,
And gives herself up to the fire
—Though her sins in hundreds aggregate—
Straight to heaven she will go,
With her departed spouse in tow.'

The chariot-maker heard all this. 'I am blessed indeed,' he said to himself, 'to have such a wife who speaks so lovingly of her husband, and is so devoted to him.' And with this thought in mind, he picked up the bed, with the couple still in it, upon his head and danced, full of joy."

~

The crane continued his narrative. 'I was then offered the usual courtesies by the king, and dismissed. The parrot too is on his way here. Let arrangements now be made for whatever needs to be done after considering all these developments.'

The swan king's minister, the goose, smiled and said, 'Sire, the crane has attended to official business as best as he could, even while he was travelling abroad. But, sire, this is the nature of fools. For,

> A hundred times one should give way   (31)
> But not quarrel, wise men say;
> Without a cause to still dispute—
> This is but a fool's pursuit.'

'What is the point of criticizing the past?' said the king, 'Let us prepare for what is before us.' The goose replied: 'Sire, I will speak in private. For,

> From change of colour of the visage,   (32)
> From shifting gaze and body language,
> And from the voice's resonance,
> The wise can often gauge the sense.
> So, one should exchange advice
> In private, far from prying eyes.'

The others then withdrew, while the king and the minister remained. The goose said, 'Sire, I believe that the crane has done this at the instigation of some other officer. For,

> Doctors love the man who's ailing,   (33)
> And officers him who has some failing.
> Clever folk on fools survive,
> But goodness keeps the good alive.'

'That may be so,' said the king, 'but we can investigate these reasons later. For the present, let us see what is to be done now.'

The goose said, 'Sire, let a spy go there first. Then we will get to know their organization and their strengths and weaknesses. For,

> What should be done or not, to see (34)
> At home or in a foreign state,
> A spy the sovereign's eyes must be,
> Or else blindness is his fate.

'Let the spy go with another trustworthy person. Then he can stay there, secretly ascertain the local plans, explain them to his assistant, and send him back. As it is said,

> While hearing religious dissertations (35)
> In temples, convents or in shrines,
> The king should hold his consultations
> With agents disguised as divines.

'A secret spy is one who can move on both land and water. So appoint this very crane. And let another crane like him go as his deputy. Their families should be kept hostage at the palace gate. But sire, all this should be arranged very secretly. For,

> If private consultations do (36)
> Get shared by people more than two,
> They then become no better than
> Public news for every man.
> Therefore such discussions kingly
> Should be held with others singly.

'Look,

> Those adept in policy (37)
> Say there is no remedy
> For evils which a leak will bring
> From the counsels of the king.'

'Well,' said the king after reflection, 'I certainly have the best spy.' 'Then you also have victory in war,' the minster replied. Meanwhile the gatekeeper entered, saluted, and said, 'Sire, a parrot has come from Jambu island, and stands at the gate.'

The king looked at the goose. 'Let him first be taken to the residence prepared for him,' the goose said, 'he will be sent for and seen later.' The gatekeeper then withdrew to conduct the parrot to his quarters.

'Well, war is upon us,' said the king. 'Even so, sire,' the goose replied, 'to decide post-haste on war is not wise. For,

Is he aide or minister true, (38)
At the very outset who,
Without having given thought,
Advises that his sovereign ought
To get ready for a war,
Or from his own land withdraw?

'Furthermore,

To vanquish enemies one should try, (39)
But never by the means of war.
For in that case, of victory,
Neither party can be sure.

'Further,

Enemies one should influence (40)
By measures conciliatory,
By gifts, or stoking dissidence;
By one of these, or all the three
Used together, to be sure;
But never by resort to war.

'For,

Everyone's a hero sure, (41)
As long as he's not in a war.
As long as he does not know
The true power of the foe,
Who will not a braggart be,
Full of pride and vanity?

'What is more,

Men cannot as easily (42)
Lift a rock as it can be
Levered with a piece of wood.
Consultations also should
By little means gain ends immense—
This is their greatest consequence.

'But, seeing that war may be imminent, one should also make preparations. For,

Like in a farm, in policy (43)
The fruit cannot come instantly—
It needs timely labour done
For results, sire, to be won.

'Furthermore,

Fear of danger when it's distant, (44)
But true valour in its instant:
Great men have this quality.
In times of a calamity
The great ones of this world display
Steadfast courage all the way.

'Further,

In success of every kind (45)

The obstacle most primary
Is excitation of the mind.
Does not one, for instance, see
That even water, icy cold[4],
Pierces through the mountain fold?

'And specially, sire, as this King Dapple is very powerful.
For,

It has been ordained nowhere   (46)
That with the strong one must have war.
If man will fight an elephant here,
He will perish, it is sure.

'Further

He is a fool who goes to war   (47)
Without an opportunity.
To fight the mighty, it is sure,
Is flapping wings just like a bee.

'What is more,

Some blows one should even take   (48)
And stay contracted, tortoise-like.
But when the time comes, like a snake
The statesman rises, fierce, to strike.

'Listen, sire,

One skilled in all expedient   (49)
Is equally then competent
The big and small to extirpate,
Just as a river in full spate
Submerges both grass and tree,
Each with equal facility.

'So let this ambassador, the parrot, be assured and detained till our fortress has been made ready. For,

> One archer on its wall fights back (50)
> A hundred sent forth to attack.
> A hundred on the battlement
> Can match a hundred thousand sent.
> This is why the wise declare
> That one should a fort prepare.

> Without a fort, whose territory (51)
> Will not to foes defenceless be?
> Like one shipwrecked, without support,
> Is a king who has no fort.

> Equipped with moats and ramparts high, (52)
> Mechanical aids, a water supply,
> Midst mountains one should forts locate,
> Or deserts and forests desolate.

> An extremely rough terrain, (53)
> Proper egress and access,
> Stores of water, fuel, grain,
> Space, and due extensiveness—
> Seven precious properties
> Of a fortress are all these.'

'Who should be assigned to get the fort ready?' asked the king. The goose said, 'Call the stork, because

> For each trade that man should be used (54)
> Who has in it full competence.
> Even the learned are confused
> When they lack experience.'

This was done, and when the stork arrived, the king looked

at him and said, 'O stork, prepare a fort immediately.' The stork saluted and replied, 'Sire, I had long ago marked out this great lake itself for a fortress. Necessary materials should be stored on the island at its centre. And

> Of all the things that should be stored (55)
> The best, O King, is edible grain.
> For jewels and suchlike though one hoard,
> One cannot eat to life sustain.

'What is more,

> Of all the spices that there are, (56)
> It's known that salt is best by far.
> Lacking it, upon the tongue
> All sauces taste like cattle dung.'

'Go quickly, and arrange everything,' the king ordered the stork. Meanwhile the gatekeeper came in again and announced, 'Sire, a chief of the crows named Meghavarna or Cloudcolour has arrived from Simhala island, and stands at the gate with his retinue. He wishes to meet Your Majesty.'

'A crow, too, sees a lot and knows every thing,' observed the king, 'so he deserves to be kept with us.'

'That is so, sire,' said the goose. 'But the crow is a land bird. He is from the side of our enemies. How can he be kept with us? As has been said,

> The fool who will with enemies stay (57)
> Forsaking his party true—
> Him the other side will slay
> Like the jackal coloured blue.'

'How did that happen?' the king asked. The minister narrated

The Blue Jackal

There was a jackal from the forest who fell into a vat of blue dye while wandering about the outskirts of a town. Unable to come out, he pretended to be dead when he was still inside next morning. He was then pulled out by the owner of the vat who, believing that this was a dead animal, took him to some distance and threw him down, whereupon he ran away.

Back in the forest, when the jackal saw that his body had turned blue, he said to himself, 'I now have a most excellent colour. Why should I then not obtain some advancement for myself?' Having considered this, he summoned all the other jackals, and told them, 'The blessed goddess of the woods has with her own hands anointed me with the juices of all the herbs as the king of this forest. From today, therefore, all business in the forest should be done only as I command.'

Observing the jackal's distinctive colouration, the other jackals prostrated themselves in homage before him. 'As you command, sire,' they said, and in the same way his sovereignty came to be acknowledged by all the animals who lived in the forest.

Surrounded by his kinsfolk, the jackal soon gained supreme power. But, having acquired the noblest of animals, like the tiger and the lion, as his servants, he was ashamed to see other jackals in his court. So he spurned them, and sent his kin away.

The other jackals were deeply distressed. Seeing them in this condition, an ancient jackal spoke up. 'Do not be dejected. This animal does not know what is in his own interest. If we, who understand statecraft and know his weaknesses, have been spurned by him, then we too should do something which will bring about his destruction. The tiger and the others consider him as their king only because they have been deceived by his colour. They do not realize that he is no more than a jackal. So, we should have him exposed.

'This is what should be done. In the evening all of you should set up a loud howl in unison near him. On hearing it, he too is bound to follow the nature of his species and do the same. For,

> Its always hard for any creature   (58)
> To go against its basic nature;
> A dog can be crowned king, it's true,
> But will it cease to gnaw a shoe?

'Recognized by his howls, he is then bound to be killed by the tiger.'

And this is exactly what happened. As it is said:

> When your kin becomes a foe,   (59)
> All your secrets he does know—
> Your weaknesses and strengths entire.
> He can burn you like the fire
> Sparked inside a withered tree,
> To incinerate it utterly.

~

'That is why I spoke about the fool who forsakes his own side,' the goose concluded. 'That is so,' said the king, 'still the crow should be received as he has come from far away. We can consider later if he should be kept here.'

The goose said, 'Sire, our spy has been despatched, and our fortress prepared. Let the parrot also be dismissed after you have seen him. But,

> Cāṇakya did Nanda destroy[5]   (60)
> By using a skilled envoy

The king should meet an emissary
In brave but sober company.'

An assembly was then held, and the parrot and the crow summoned to it. The parrot, his head held rather high, assumed the seat offered to him and stated, 'O Goldegg, the great king His Majesty Dapple commands you, "If you care for your life and your wealth, come immediately and bow before our feet. Otherwise think of living somewhere else."'

The king was enraged. 'Aah!' he cried, 'is not there anyone in our assembly who will catch this creature by the neck?' Cloudcolour stood up and said, 'Command me, sire! I will kill this vile parrot.' Knowall pacified the king and the crow, saying, 'First listen:

A council true it cannot be   (61)
Which lacks men of maturity.
And no man can be called mature
Who speaks not that which is the law.
Law cannot be of truth remiss.
To verge on fraud: no truth is this.

'And the law is that:

An outcaste though the envoy be,   (62)
From death he has immunity.
For he is but his sovereign's voice,
And in speech he has no choice,
Even if the enemy raise
The sword on every word he says.

'Furthermore,

If and when an envoy says   (63)
Words which are in one's dispraise,

Or he lauds the enemy,
Whoever takes that seriously?
All kinds of things ambassadors rant,
Their status being sacrosanct.'

The king and the crow then calmed down. The parrot also
got up and withdrew, but he was brought back by the goose,
and presented gold ornaments and other gifts with suitable
words before he was seen off.

The parrot returned to the Vindhyā mountain and saluted
his king. On seeing him, King Dapple asked, 'Parrot, what
is the news? What is that country like?' The parrot said,
'Sire, the news in brief is that we must now prepare for
war. As for that country, how can I describe it? It is like a
bit of paradise.'

The king then summoned all his councillors and sat down
to deliberate with them. 'We have now to go to war,' he
said. 'Give your advice as to how this should be done. But
war there has to be, that is quite certain. For,

> For kings its ruin to be sated,   (64)
> As for priests to yearn for more,
> For ladies to be shameless rated,
> For courtesans to turn demure.'

The vulture, who was named Dūrdarśī or Farsighted, spoke
up. 'Sire, it is not advisable to make war in unfavourable
circumstances. For,

> When your friends, well-wishers and   (65)
> Aides in firm devotion stand,
> And the case is to the contrary
> In camps of your adversary—
> That is then the moment for
> Marching out and making war.

'Further,

> Allies, gold and territory: (66)
> Of war are these the benefits three.
> Of gaining them if you are sure
> Only then should you make war.'

'Let the minster first review my forces,' said the king, 'so that their fitness may be judged. Let the soothsayer also be called to determine and tell us an auspicious time to march out.'

'Even so,' said the minister, 'it is not good to be in a hurry to march out. For,

> The fools who rashly choose to face (67)
> The enemy's force without due thought,
> It is but his sword's embrace
> That for certain they have got.'

'Minister!' the king exclaimed, 'do not keep demoralizing me. Tell me how someone wanting to win should attack another's territory.' 'I will,' said the vulture, 'but this will give results only if carried out as explained. As it is said,

> As with the holy writ, O King, (68)
> Can counsel any benefit bring,
> If it is not carried out?
> Mere knowledge of the remedy
> Will never cure a malady—
> Of this can there be any doubt?

'But the king's command cannot be disregarded, and I will relate what I have learnt. Listen,

> River, mountain pass or wood— (69)
> Wherever, O King, threats may lie,

To each such point the general should
Go forth with forces, speedily.

The captain should march in the van, (70)
And with him every fighting man.
King, treasure and seraglio—
At the centre these should go,
With those who have a lesser role
In the army as a whole.

On both the wings there ought to be (71)
Deployment of the cavalry,
And on either side of horses,
There should be the chariot forces.
Next to them the elephants put,
And then the men who fight on foot.

The general should bring up the rear (72)
With councillors and troops select,
Marching slowly, giving cheer
To the weary; in effect
He should, O King, the army serve
As its backup and reserve.

Difficult hill or marsh terrain, (73)
Using elephants one should force;
With horses that which is more plain;
With boats ford rivers, and of course
Every kind of territory
Can be crossed with infantry.

To march by elephant, it is said, (74)
Is best when rains begin to spread.
In other seasons, use the horse,
And infantry year-round, of course.

On mountain roads and passes grim, (75)
The monarch well-protected keep
With sturdy soldiers guarding him;
Still, he should but lightly sleep.

Harass and destroy the foe (76)
By strikes through forest territory.
When you into his country go,
In front let jungle tribesmen be.

Wherever may the sovereign be, (77)
There should be kept his treasury,
From which his own retainers may
Be given what is due as pay.
Men will for paymasters fight,
But no treasure means no sovereign right.

'For,

Man is not of man a slave— (78)
He's money's slave, Your Majesty.
His being great or just a knave
Comes from wealth or poverty.

Troops should fight unitedly, (79)
Guarding one another's way;
And infirm soldiers if there be,
Should in the column's centre stay.

In the vanguard of his force, (80)
The king his ground troops should locate;
A siege upon his foes enforce,
Laying waste their land and state.

One should fight upon a plain (81)
With chariots and with cavalry;

With boats and elephants on terrain
Which is all marsh or watery;
With the bow in forests, and
With sword and shield on open land.

Always spoil the foe's supply (82)
Of fodder, food and energy.
His water tanks destroy, and do
The same to moats and ramparts too.

The elephant is the force's head— (83)
O King, it has no substitute.
Its very limbs, it has been said,
Are weapons eight[5] of great repute.

The horse is every army's might, (84)
It's like a rampart which can move.
On land that king will win a fight
Whose cavalry does better prove.

'And, as it is said,

Equestrian fighters, in a war, (85)
Even the gods find hard to beat.
Enemies, though still distant, for
Them are as if at their feet.

It's said to be infantry's role (86)
To guard the army as a whole,
To keep the roads on all sides free,
And in attack the first to be.

That force is said to be the best, (87)
Whose valour is by nature blest,
Whose men are skilled in weaponry,
Forever firm in loyalty,

With endurance built to last,
And mainly from the warrior caste.

As men on earth will fight for fame   (88)
And honour from their master sought,
O King, they never do the same
For money only, though a lot.

Better have a smaller force   (89)
Formed of men of quality,
Than muster up a great concourse
Of as many heads as there can be.
For, if the weak do break in war,
The strong will break with them, it's sure.

Not awarding honours due,   (90)
And removing leaders true,
Confiscations from the pay,
Lack of redress, and delay—
This can be the leading source
Of disaffection in a force.

The troops of one's adversary   (91)
Can be destroyed easily
When they have been tired out
By marches long and roundabout.
But one who seeks a victory
Should attack the enemy
While ensuring that his own
Forces have not weary grown.

To disunite the enemy   (92)
There is no better strategy
Than to use one of his kin.
Therefore put all efforts in
Setting up against the foe

A rival claimant from below.

A clear-headed invader must   (93)
Promote internal lack of trust,
Allying with his enemy's heir,
Or the chief minister there.

War-like allies of the foe   (94)
Should be extirpated so:
By destruction in a war,
By seizing of their cattle, or
By taking action to detain
Their officers and servants main.

The king his lands should colonize   (95)
With settlers brought in from outside
By force, or with some gift or prize—
For settled land does wealth provide.'

'Why talk so much?' said the king, 'for,

One's own rise, the other's fall: (96)
All policy is in essence
These two ends, which experts all
Admit despite their eloquence.'

'All this is true,' the minister replied with a smile, 'but,

Power which is arbitrary,   (97)
And that which law and scriptures guide,
To each other are contrary
And cannot in one place reside.
Where can one for instance see
A place both dark and light to be?'

The king then arose to march out at the auspicious hour

proposed by the soothsayers.

Meanwhile the messenger despatched by Goldegg's spy also returned, saying, 'Sire, King Dapple is almost here. He is now encamped with his army on the plateau of the Malaya mountain. Our fort needs to be kept under constant surveillance, for that vulture is a formidable minister. I have come to know of his confidential talk with someone about his secret plan. According to it some person has already been placed by him inside our fort.'

The goose said, 'Sire, this can only be the crow.'

'Never!' said the king, 'If that were so, why should he have tried to have the parrot punished? Moreover, he has been here for a while, and it is only after the parrot left that we have started anticipating war.'

'Nevertheless strangers have to be suspected,' the minister said. 'Sometimes even strangers turn out to be helpful,' the king replied. 'Listen,

> One who helps you is your brother,   (98)
> Though a stranger he may be.
> And one who harms is just another,
> Though he share fraternity.
> Born of your own body's frame,
> Illness hurts you all the same,
> While healing herbs will benefits show,
> Though they in distant forests grow.

'Furthermore

> In King Śūdraka's retinue   (99)
> Was Vīravara, a servant who
> Within no time, while he was there,
> Sacrificed his son and heir.'

'How did that happen?' asked the goose. The king narrated

The Faithful Servant

'There was a time when I was in love with Karpūra Manjarī, the daughter of the royal swan Karpūrakeli, who lived at the pleasure lake of King Śūdraka. Once a prince named Vīravara came their from another country. Going up to the palace gate, he told the gate-keeper, "I am a prince and I am looking for employment. Let me meet the king."

When he was taken to the king, he said, "Sire, should you need me as a servant, please arrange for my wages."

"How much will they be?" Śūdraka asked. "Four hundred pieces of gold every day," replied Vīravara.

"And what do you offer?" asked the king. "My two arms," Vīravara responded, "and thirdly, my sword." "This will not do," said the king. On hearing this Vīravara bowed and withdrew.

The ministers then told the king, "Sire, employ him at this wage for four days. This will enable us to judge his worth and if his qualities deserve such a remuneration or not." In accordance with this advice he recalled Vīravara, and gave him four hundred golden pieces together with a betel leaf in token of his appointment.

The king kept secret watch on how Vīravara spent the money. Half of it the new servant gave for the gods and the priests. Of the remainder, he gave half to the poor, and spent the rest on articles of consumption or on amusements. Apart from this daily routine, he attended night and day at the palace gate, his sword in his hand. He would go home only when the king himself ordered it.

Once it was a dark and moonless night. King Śūdraka heard the sound of a piteous weeping. "Is there anyone at the door?" he cried. "Sire, it is I, Vīravara," came the reply. "Find out what this weeping is about," ordered the king. "As you command, sire," said Vīravara, and he marched out.

"This is not proper," thought the king, "I have sent that

prince out alone into the pitch-black darkness. I should follow him to see what this is." And he too picked up a sword and followed the other man out of the city.

Going ahead, Vīravara at last saw a woman weeping. She was young and beautiful, and adorned with all kinds of ornaments. "Who are you," he asked her, "why are you weeping?"

"I am the Sovereignty of this King Śūdraka," the woman said. "I have rested for long in great comfort under the shadow of his arms. But now I must go elsewhere."

"When there is a problem there must also be a solution," said Vīravara. "What should be done so that Your Ladyship continues to reside here?"

"Your son Śaktidhara bears the thirty-two auspicious marks on his body," said Sovereignty, "if you will sacrifice him to the goddess Sarvamangalā then I can continue to live here for long." Having uttered these words, she disappeared.

Vīravara then went home and woke up his sleeping wife and son. After they had got up and taken their seats, he told them all that Sovereignty had said. Having heard it, Śaktidhara said happily, "I am blessed indeed that I can be of service for safeguarding the dominion of our master. Father, what is now the need for delay? The utilization of this body, for this purpose and in this manner, is always esteemed. For,

For others sake, a person wise   (100)
Will life and money sacrifice.
Its better to renounce them for
A good cause when their end is sure."

"If this is not done," added Śaktidhara's mother, "then how else will you give return for this enormous salary?"

After deliberating upon this they all proceeded to the temple of Sarvamangalā. There Vīravara prayed to the deity, and said, "O goddess, be gracious! May the great King

Śūdraka always be victorious! Accept this offering!" And, with these words, he cut off his son's head.

Vīravara then said to himself, "The wages I took from the king have now been repaid. But my life will be a mockery without my son." Thinking thus, he cut off his own head also. His wife, distraught with grief for her husband and her son, followed suit.

The king had been a witness to all this. Full of wonder, he said to himself,

> "Petty creatures such as I   (101)
> Merely live and merely die.
> One such as him was never seen
> Nor will be on this earthly scene.

"My kingdom too is useless now that he has passed away from it." Then Śūdraka also drew his sword to decapitate himself. At that moment the goddess Sarvamangalā herself appeared and held back the king's hand. "My son," she said, "I am pleased with you. Do not be so impetuous. Nothing will happen to your kingdom even after your life ends."

The king prostrated himself in the eightfold[7] obeisance. "Goddess!" he cried, "what is the use of my kingdom or even of my life? If I deserve your compassion, then, with whatever remains of the life span ordained for me, let Vīravara live again with his spouse and his son. Otherwise let me follow my destiny."

"My son, I am entirely satisfied by your magnanimity and your love for your servants. Go and prosper. This prince and his family will also live again." With these words, the goddess vanished. Vīravara, his son and his spouse were restored to life, and went home. Unobserved by them, the king also returned to the inner apartment of the palace and went to bed.

Later, when Vīravara was back at the gate, he was again

questioned by the king. "Sire," he said, "the woman who
was weeping vanished on seeing me. Nothing else happened
at all." The king was content on hearing these words. But
he marvelled and said to himself. "How praiseworthy is this
great personage! For,

> Rich, he always sweetly speaks;   (102)
> Brave, he does not ever boast;
> Strong but tender, and he seeks
> To give where it is needed most.

"These are the signs of a great man, and he has them all."

The next morning the king held an assembly of his nobles,
narrated all that had happened, and rewarded Vīravara with
the kingdom of Karṇāṭa.

~

'So how can someone be considered a villain just because
he is a stranger?' said the swan king. 'Among strangers too
there are the good, the bad, and the indifferent.' The goose
responded,

> 'In keeping with his sovereign's whim,   (103)
> One who will commend to him
> Something which he should not do
> As a course of action true—
> Is that a minister good?
> Far better that the master should
> Be displeased, than be destroyed
> By doing what he should avoid.

> When physicians and priests of kings   (104)
> Tell them only pleasant things,
> Their health and virtue soon will be

Lost; so too their treasury,
If their ministers also tell
Only what may please them well.

'Listen, sire,

"What someone got by religious merit,   (105)
I must also try to get it."
Thinking thus, the barber, who
Sought wealth and was greedy too,
Killed a mendicant for one,
And then himself to death was done.'

'How did that happen?' asked the king. The minister narrated

The Greedy Barber

*I*n the city of Ayodhya there was a man of the warrior caste named Ćūdamaṇi. He wanted to acquire wealth and, inflicting many tortures upon himself, he prayed for a long time to the god who wears the crescent moon as a crest jewel. After his sins had been cleansed, at the god's command, the lord of the Yakshas[8] appeared to him in a dream and said, 'This morning, after you have shaved, take a cudgel in your hand and hide besides the door of your house. Then, whichever mendicant you see coming into the courtyard, hit him mercilessly with the cudgel. The mendicant will turn into a pot full of gold at that very moment, and with that treasure you can live happily for the rest of your life.'

Ćūdamaṇi did as he had been told, with results as had been predicted. All this was witnessed by the barber who had been called to shave him. 'Here is a fine method for getting hold of a treasure,' said the barber to himself. 'Why should I not do the same?'

From then onwards, the barber would stand similarly, hidden with a cudgel in his hand, awaiting the arrival of a mendicant. Eventually one appeared, and the barber struck him so hard that he died. The king's officers punished the barber for this crime, and he too lost his life.

~

'That is why I mentioned getting something which can only be had by religious merit,' said the minister. The king observed:

'How can one a stranger know,   (106)
Just by tales of actions past,
Whether he'll true friendship show,
Or a traitor turn at last?

'But let that be. Let us attend to what is before us. If Dapple is on the Malaya plateau, what should now be done?'

'Sire,' said the minister, 'I have learnt from the spy who has returned that Dapple has shown no respect for the advice of his great minister, the vulture. He can, as such, be defeated, for he is a fool. As it is said:

'Greedy, cruel, careless too,   (107)
Unstable, timid, and untrue,
A fool, who's lazy, and will not
Respect his soldiers as he ought—
It's said that such an enemy
Can be vanquished easily.

'Therefore let the stork and our other generals be ordered to destroy his forces on the river, mountain and forest roads before he can besiege our fort, As it is said:

'With long marches worn and tired,   (108)
In rivers, hills or forests mired,

By fear of conflagrations pressed,
By hunger and by thirst distressed;

A mob, with numbers on the wane, (109)
Disorganized by storm and rain,
Stressed by famine and disease,
Or careless, caught in festivities;

Stuck in water, mud or sands, (110)
Scattered, chased by robber bands;
When the enemy force is so—
For a kill the king should go.

'Further,

He should keep the foe awake (111)
By fear of sorties he will make,
And when the soldiers doze by day,
Those sleepy heads the king should slay.

'So let our commanders go whenever there is an opportunity,
night or day, and destroy the forces of that blunderer.'

This was done, and many of Dapple's generals and
soldiers perished. A dejected Dapple then said to his minister,
Farsighted, 'Why are you neglecting me, Father? Has there
been any lapse my part? As it is said,

Just because of sovereignty, (112)
One should not be arrogant.
Such conduct ends prosperity,
Like age does beauty excellent.

'Further,

Able men do wealth obtain, (113)
Light eaters their health regain,

Healthy people happy stay,
The diligent master learning's way,
And those with tact and courtesy
Earn merit, fame and prosperity.'

'Listen, sire,' the vulture replied,

Just as trees which grow beside   (114)
And flourish by the waterside,
So too, monarchs who have not
Any wit or learning got,
Still can win prosperity
By always keeping company
With those who have matured with time
To wisdom ripe and most sublime.

Wine and women, games of chance,   (115)
Hunting and extravagance,
Words and deeds of cruelty—
Vices are of royalty.

The greatest gains will not be won   (116)
By deeds of daring rashly done,
Nor by minds which continue
To ponder over what to do.
But success there is bound to be
In prudence joined to bravery.

'After observing the enthusiasm of your army, you
concentrated only on acts of daring. You used strong
language, and paid no attention to the advice which even I
had submitted. You therefore see the results of wrong policy.
As it is said:

Who does not, with advice bad,   (117)
Have problems in his policies?

Unwholesome diet who has had,
And not suffered some fell disease?
Whom does not wealth make arrogant?
Whom does not death destroy?
Whoever can escape torment
From the wiles women employ?

'Furthermore,

Sorrow does all joy negate;   (118)
The first snowfall, autumnal beauty;
The shining sun, the night's dark state;
Ingratitude, the virtuous duty;
Gaining something cherished, gloom;
Wise policies, calamity;
And wrong conduct does spell the doom
Of even great prosperity.

'Then I too told myself that this king has no discrimination.
Else why should he let the clear moonlight of policy precepts
be obscured by verbal fireworks? For,

What can learning do for man   (119)
When he lacks intelligence?
It is as if a mirror can
To someone blind make any sense.

'That is why I too kept silent.'
The king then clasped his hands together and said: 'I
was at fault, Father. Please forgive me, and now advise as
to how I may extricate the remainder of my army and go
back to the Vindhyā mountain.'
'I must respond to this,' the vulture said to himself, 'for,

In all dealings with royalty,   (120)
With the gods and one's guru,

> With children and the elderly,
> With holy cows and clerics too,
> And with those to sickness prey—
> Anger should be kept at bay.'

He then smiled and told the king, 'Sire, have no fear. Be assured. Listen,

> The minister's mind and quality (121)
> It seen when projects go askew,
> As the physician's you may see
> When maladies descend on you.
> Who can skill and wisdom tell
> When everything is going well?

'Furthermore,

> The little efforts small minds make (122)
> Fluster them exceedingly.
> Great tasks the resolute undertake
> And pursue them with constancy.

'With just Your Majesty's grace, therefore, I will storm the enemy's fortress and soon take you back to the Vindhya mountain with all power and glory.'

'How can this be done now, with our depleted force?' asked the king.

'Everything will be done, sire,' said the vulture. 'For one who seeks victory, prompt action is a sure guarantee of success. Therefore let the fortress gate be invested straightaway.'

~

Meanwhile the crane sent out to spy returned and told

Goldegg, 'Sire, though King Dapple has only a small force, he has come forward on the strength of the vulture's advice, and is about to invest the gate of our fort.'

'What should be done now, Knowall?' asked the swan king. The goose said, 'Let a determination be made of the strong and the weak people in our force. After ascertaining this, let gifts of gold, garments and the like be distributed in accordance with merit. For,

> One who even guards a cent (123)
> From ever being wrongly spent,
> As if a hoard of gold it were;
> But will spending millions dare
> When circumstances so demand,
> And do it with an open hand—
> The goddess of prosperity
> Will never leave one such as he.

'Further,

> On these eight, there is no such thing (124)
> As overspending, O Great King:
> Weddings, and fire ceremonies;
> Weakening one's enemies;
> Times of some calamity;
> Acts to win celebrity;
> The gaining of a loyal friend;
> Or a woman one loves no end;
> And welfare of one's kin and kith
> Who have naught to subsist with.

'For,

> Fearing but a small expense, (125)
> The fool forsakes the greater prize.
> Will a man with any sense

Give up all his merchandise
Out of an excessive care
For the tax that he must bear?'

'How can a large expenditure be proper at this time?' the king asked. 'It is said:

"Save money for some difficulty."'   (126)
'How can one for kings there be?' the minister
responded.
'For money goeth here and there,' the king continued.
'Though hoarded, it will disappear,' the minister
concluded.

'Therefore, sire, give up this parsimony and let your able warriors be rewarded with gifts and honours. As it is said,

With zeal and camaraderie rife,   (127)
Pledged full and firm to give up life—
If treated well, these noble men
Will vanquish every enemy then.

'Furthermore,

Even five times hundred bold   (128)
Warriors, made in merit's mould,
Resolute, united in their role,
Can rout an enemy army whole.

'What's more,

Eminent men of noble station,   (129)
No less than those of common state,
Shun him who has no discrimination,
Is brusque and selfish, an ingrate.

'For,

> Truth and valour, mercy and   (130)
> Munificence with open hand:
> Of any king or ruler these
> Are the chiefest qualities.
> One without them will obtain
> Only censure in his reign.

'It is necessary, moreover, that the ministers themselves be rewarded on such an occasion. As it has been said,

> One whose rise and fall is bound   (131)
> With yours, who has been trusty found:
> Such a one should be assigned
> Your person and your wealth to mind.

'For,

> If the king's ministers be   (132)
> Rogues, or women, or too young,
> By winds of faulty policy
> He will be so tossed and flung,
> That he will drown with all his cares
> In the sea of state affairs.

'Listen, sire,

> To him the earth yields wealth for sure,   (133)
> Whose joy and wrath are circumspect,
> Who has full faith in holy law,
> And treats his servants with respect.

> Never should the king despise   (134)
> His ministers, for it's known
> That their fortunes fall or rise

For certain with his very own.

'For,

> A king gone blind with vanity (135)
> Who falls into the fearful sea
> Of the problems of his land,
> Will always find a helping hand
> In such actions as depend
> On an aide who is a friend.'

Meanwhile Cloudcolour the crow had come forward. 'Your attention, sire,' he said, saluting. 'The enemy is at the fortress gate, seeking battle. With Your Majesty's permission I shall march out and demonstrate my valour. In this way I will also be able to repay the debt I owe to Your Majesty.'

'Not like this!' said the goose. 'If one has to go out and fight, the protection afforded by the fort itself becomes pointless. Furthermore,

> The alligator does one scare, (136)
> But, outside its watery lair,
> Even it can be controlled.
> And the lion too, so bold,
> When outside its jungle home,
> Like a jackal does become.

'Sire, you should go yourself and see the battle. For,

> Putting his soldiers to the fore, (137)
> The king should oversee them in war.
> When by their own master led,
> Even dogs like lions tread.'

Then they all went to the gate of the fortress and made a mighty battle.

~

On the following day King Dapple said to the vulture, 'Father, it is now time that you fulfilled your promise.'

'Sire,' replied the vulture, 'first listen,

These in a fort are said to be   (138)
The points of vulnerability:
If it be small or insecure,
Or lacks the will to long endure,
Or be by timid soldiers manned,
With fools or scoundrels in command.

'But none of these conditions obtain in this case.

Still, it is said that there are four   (139)
Methods to take a fort in war:
A secret deal, a long blockade,
Great valour, and an escalade.

'And I will make an effort as best as possible in this direction,' the vulture whispered into the king's ear. 'It will be thus . . .'

~

Then, as the battle commenced at all the four gates of the fort even before sunrise, the crows simultaneously set fire to the houses inside. There were shouts that the fort had been taken. Hearing the tumult, and seeing many houses actually ablaze with fire, the swan king's soldiers and other inhabitants of the fort quickly jumped into the lake. For,

Be it counsel, heroic feat,   (140)
Swift attack or quick retreat,
When the time is ripe, one ought
To act, not stay immersed in thought.

Goldegg the swan king was easy-going by nature. As he
proceeded slowly, accompanied by the stork, he was attacked
by Dapple's general, the rooster. 'General Stork!' he cried
out to his companion, 'do not get yourself killed for my
sake. You can still escape. Go and jump into the water and
save yourself. Make my son Ćudamaṇi, that is Crestjewel,
the king after consulting Knowall.'

'Sire! You must not utter such unbearable words!' the
stork replied. 'May you stay victorious as long as the sun
and the moon stay in the sky. Sire, I am the keeper of this
fort. The enemy will come through its gate only over my
dead body. Furthermore, sire,

Patient, kind, on merit set: (141)
Such masters are hard to get.'

'That is indeed true,' said the king, 'but,

Honest, skilled, of loyal mind:
Such servants too are hard to find.'

'Hear me further, sire,' the stork continued.

'If, by running away from war,   (142)
The fear of death would be no more,
It would then be proper to
Leave from here for some place new.
But, death being a certain feature
On earth for every living creature,
Why should we, in this situation,

Spoil in vain our fair reputation?

'Further,

> Like foam upon a wave wind-tossed,   (143)
> Life does but for a moment last.
> If it is for others lost,
> It's only due to merits past.

> The king, the minister, and the land,   (144)
> Fortress, treasury, army, and
> Allies, subjects, citizenry—
> A kingdom's limbs are said to be.

'You are our master, sire, and you must be protected in every way. For,

> Subjects of their lord deprived,   (145)
> Though prosperous, have not survived.
> Can physicians, though from heaven sent,
> Do anything when life is spent?

'Furthermore,

> People bloom when their kings shine,   (146)
> And fade with sovereigns in decline—
> It's like the lotus and the sun,
> When morning comes or day is done.'

Meanwhile the rooster had come forward and struck the swan king hard with his sharp claws. The stork advanced swiftly, and covered the king with his own body. Battered by blows from the rooster's beak and claws, he kept the king covered with his own limbs, and pushed him into the water. Finally, he killed the rooster with a blow of his beak, but was himself surrounded by many others and slain.

Thereafter King Dapple entered the fortress and had the treasures inside it taken away. Delighted by the victory chants of his bards, he then returned to his own camp.

~

$\mathcal{T}$he princes said, 'The stork was the only one with merit in that king's army. He protected his master at the cost of his own life. It has been said:

> Most calves which mother cows deliver,   (147)
> Are just plain cattle, that is all.
> Seldom one turns out, if ever,
> With horns that sweep its shoulders tall—
> Not a common beast, recurred,
> But a leader of the herd.'

Viṣṇu Śarma said, 'May that noble one experience the joys of heaven with celestial nymphs as his attendants. It is said,

> The brave who give their lives in war   (148)
> For their master's enterprise,
> Loyal and grateful: it is sure
> Such men will go to paradise.

> Wherever does the warrior fall,   (149)
> When encircled by the foe,
> And shows no cowardice at all,
> Straight to heaven he will go.

'Your Highnesses have now heard the topic of war.'
    'We have heard it,' said the princes, 'and we are very pleased.'
    'May this happen also,' Viṣṇu Śarma concluded,

'May kings never wage a war   (150)
With elephant, horse and infantry.
May their enemies evermore,
By winds of proper policy,
To mountain caves be swept aside,
There to take refuge and hide.'

Sandhi

Peace

*I*t was time to resume the discourse. 'Noble sir,' said the princes, 'we have learnt about war. Tell us now about peace.'

'Listen,' replied Viṣṇu Śarma, 'I will also explain *Sandhi* or Peace. This is the first stanza:

When the two kings fought a war,   (1)
And their armies were no more,
Then the vulture and the goose
Neither did a moment lose,
But, through talks mediatory,
Had peace concluded speedily.'

'How did that happen?' the princes asked. Viṣṇu Śarma continued his narrative.

'Who set fire to our fort?' asked the swan king. 'Was it done by the enemy, or by someone living in the fort who was instigated by the other side?'

'Sire,' the goose replied, 'Your Majesty's sudden well-wisher Cloudcolour has disappeared with his retinue. So I believe that this must have been his work.'

The king thought for some time, and said, 'That was indeed my bad luck, As it is said:

Ministers are not to blame,   (2)
It is the fault of destiny.
A work well planned will all the same
Fail, if fated so to be.'

'This too is said,' observed the minster,

> 'When struck by some adversity,   (3)
> A person blames his destiny,
> But the fool does not realize,
> The fault in his own action lies.

'Furthermore,

> One who does not gladly heed   (4)
> The words of friends who wish him well,
> That fool ends as did indeed
> The tortoise who from his perch fell.'

'How did that happen?' the king asked. The minister narrated

The Foolish Tortoise

There is a lake called Phullotpala in the land of Magadha. Two swans named Sankata or Narrow and Vikata or Broad had lived there since long. Their friend, a tortoise named Kambugriva or Shellneck also lived their.

Once some fishermen came to the lake and said, 'We will stay here today, and catch the fish, the tortoises and the others in the morning.' On hearing this the tortoise told the swans, 'Friends, you heard what the fishermen were saying. What should I do now?'

'Let us first make sure of this once again,' the swans replied. 'In the morning we will do whatever is appropriate.'

'No,' said the tortoise, 'I see danger in this. As it has been stated,

> The planner for contingency,   (5)
> The thinker with alacrity,
> Both did live most happily;
> But one who would say: "What will be

Will be," was ruined utterly.'

'How did that happen?' the two swans asked. The tortoise narrated

The Three Fish

*I*n the old days, when fishermen had come similarly to this very lake, the matter was discussed by three fish. One of them was named Anāgata Vidhātā or Contingency Planner. He said, "As for myself, I will go to another lake," and he went away accordingly. Another fish named Pratyutpannamati or Quick-wit said, "Where should I go, when there is no knowing what may happen. So, when the time comes, I will do whatever is appropriate. As it is said,

> The intelligent man is he   (6)
> Who surmounts calamity
> Even as it comes to be,
> Just as the merchant's wife, so wise,
> Made sure he would not recognize
> Her lover, caught before his eyes."

"How did that happen?" asked the third fish, Yadbhaviṣhya or Fatalist. Quick-wit narrated

The Quick-witted Wife

*I*n Vikramapura there was a merchant named Samudra Datta. His wife Ratnaprabhā had taken one of his servants as her lover. For,

> To womenfolk no man is dear   (7)
> Nor displeasing, it is true.
> Like cattle grazing forests bare,

They ever seek new grass to chew[1].

Once Samudra Datta caught Ratnaprabhā kissing the servant on the mouth. But the strumpet quickly went up to her husband, and said, 'Lord, this servant is much too fond off luxuries. He steals and eats our camphor. I have discovered this by smelling his mouth.' As it is said,

> Women do eat twice as much   (8)
> As men, in scriptures it is said;
> Their intelligence is four times such
> As man can have inside his head;
> Their industry is six times more,
> And eightfold is their passion's score.[2]

The servant was appalled on hearing Ratnaprabhā. 'How can any servant stay in the house of a master with such a wife,' he said, 'where the mistress wants to smell the servant's mouth every minute?' So he got up and walked out. The good merchant was able to retain him only after much effort and persuasion.

~

"That is why I talked about the intelligent person overcoming calamities as they occur," said Quick-wit. But Fatalist observed,

> "What will not, will never be,   (9)
> What will, must come to pass for sure.
> For every care this remedy;
> Why not drink, and fret no more?"[3]

When Quick-wit was caught in the net next morning, he lay still as if he were dead. On being taken out of the net, he jumped as hard as he could and dived into deep water. As for Fatalist, he was caught by the fishermen and killed.

~

'That is why I talked about the Contingency Planner and the others,' said the tortoise. 'Therefore, do something so that I may get to another lake today itself.'

'You will certainly be safe if you go to another lake,' said the swans, 'but how will you travel on land?'

'Contrive some method so that I may go with your honors by the aerial route,' the tortoise replied. 'How is that possible?' asked the swans. He said, 'I can hang by my mouth from a piece of wood you both hold up with your beaks. With the power of your wings I too will thus be able to go without difficulty.'

'This is a possible solution,' the swans said, 'but,

When of solutions think the wise,   (10)
On problems too they meditate—
Unlike the crane, before whose eyes,
The mongooses his children ate.'

'How did that happen?' the tortoise asked. The swans narrated

The Short-sighted Crane

There is a mountain called Gṛddhakūta in the northern country. Some cranes lived there on a fig tree by the side of the river Airavatī. In a burrow beneath the tree lived a serpent who was in the habit of eating the cranes' young children. On hearing the lamentations of the grief-stricken parents, another crane said, "You should do the following.

Get some fish and lay them out in a line, one by one, from the place where the mongooses live, upto this serpent's burrow. The mongooses will then come forward, attracted by the food. They are bound to see the snake, and to kill him because of the natural enmity between the two."

This was done, with the expected outcome. But the mongooses heard the chirping of the young cranes in the tree, and they climbed up and devoured them too.

~

'That is why we talked about thinking solutions through,' said the swans. 'When people see you being carried by us, they will certainly make comments. If you give any reply on hearing them, that will be your end. Therefore, all things considered, you should just stay here.'

'Am I a fool?' the tortoise exclaimed. 'I will not speak at all!' So they proceeded as planned.

All the cowherds saw the tortoise being carried in the air and ran shouting after him. 'If this tortoise falls down,' cried one, 'he should be cooked and eaten here itself.' Another said, 'He should be roasted and eaten here.' 'He should be taken home, and then consumed,' said yet another.

The tortoise became extremely angry on hearing this callous talk. Forgetting the earlier instructions, he cried out, 'Dust is what you all will eat!' And even as he spoke, he dropped down and was killed by the cowherds.

~

'That is why I spoke about heeding the words of well-meaning friends,' said the goose. Meanwhile the crane, who had been sent out as a spy, came there and said, 'Sire,

I had pointed out at the very beginning that the fort should
be kept under surveillance all the time. This you did not
do. The results of that neglect are now before us. Setting
fire to the fort was the handiwork of the crow Cloudcolour
who had been assigned to do this by the vulture.'

> The king said with a sigh:
> In enemies one who puts his trust, (11)
> Because they act affectionately,
> Or do him favours when they must,
> Is like one sleeping on a tree:
> Both will have a mighty fall
> Before they can wake up at all.'

The spy continued, 'When Cloudcolour went away from here
after setting fire to the fort, Dapple was greatly gratified.
"Let this Cloudcolour be anointed here itself as the king of
Karpūra island," he declared. "As it is said:

> A servant's work do not ignore, (12)
> Specially when he's done his chore.
> Hearten him with gifts and praise
> In thought and speech, and in your gaze."'

'And what happened then?' the goose asked. 'Then,'
continued the spy, 'the chief minister, the vulture, said,
"Sire, this will not be appropriate. Give him some other
reward. For,

> It's like giving good advice (13)
> To one who cannot understand,
> Or pounding husks which have no rice,
> Or pissing on a heap of sand.
> No durable result will show,
> O King, by favours to the low.

"Furthermore, a base person should never be appointed to an office meant for the noble. As it is said,

When high office the base obtain,   (14)
They wish to get their master slain,
As the mouse with tiger's state,
Tried the sage to obliterate."

"How did that happen?" Dapple asked. The minister narrated

The Hermit and the Mouse

In the hermitage of the great sage Gautama there was a hermit named Mahātapa. He happened to find a baby mouse which had fallen near the hermitage from the clutches of a crow. Compassionate by nature, he began to nurture the mouse with grains of wild rice.

Now a cat ran after the mouse in order to eat it, and the mouse jumped into the hermit's lap on seeing the cat. 'Mouse,' the holy man then ordained, 'become a cat.'

The cat fled on seeing a dog. 'You are scared of the dog?' said the hermit. 'Then become a dog yourself.' But the dog was afraid of a tiger, and so the hermit turned it too into a tiger.

Even though it was now a tiger, the hermit did not regard the creature as any more than a mouse. On seeing him with the tiger, all the people would also say, "This hermit changed a mouse into a tiger." The tiger was greatly vexed on hearing this talk. 'As long as this hermit lives,' he said to himself, 'this unbecoming account of my origin will also continue to be current.' Thinking thus, he set off to kill the hermit. But the latter got to know this and, decreeing, 'Become a mouse once again,' he turned the tiger back into a mouse.

"This is why I spoke about base people obtaining high office," said the minister. "Furthermore, do not think that this is easy to do. Listen,

> On many fish a crane did feast, (15)
> The great, the middling, and the least,
> Till extreme greed became the cause
> Of his demise in some crab's claws."

"How did that happen?" asked Dapple. The minister narrated

The Crane and the Crab

*I*n the Mālava land there is a lake called Padmagarbha. Once an old and decrepit crane stood there, looking extremely dejected. He was seen by a crab who asked, 'Why does Your Honour stand here without looking for any food?'

'Listen, good sir,' said the crane, 'fish are what I live on. But the news that I have heard in the city is that fishermen will come and kill them all for sure. So my death too is imminent enough with the disappearance of my natural food. Having realized this, I am not even thinking of eating.'

The fish were listening. 'At this time it seems that even he may be able to help us,' they considered. 'Let us ask him what we should do. As it is said,

> Join the helpful enemy, (16)
> Not friends who do you injury.
> For help or hindrance is the cue
> By which you know who's really who.

'O crane!' the fish then cried, 'is there any way in which we can be saved in this situation?'

'There is a way,' the crane replied. 'It is to take refuge in another lake. I can take you there, one by one.'

'Very well, then,' said the fish. The crane thereafter carried

the fish away one by one, and devoured them. In due time
the crab also asked him, 'O crane, take me there too.'

The crane coveted crab flesh which he had never tasted
before. He carried the crab with care and put him down at
a particular place. Seeing it covered with fish bones, the
crab began to worry. 'Alas, I am done for, ill fated that I
am! Very well. Now I must do what the occasion demands.
For,

> Danger one should always dread[4]   (17)
> As long as it is far away.
> But once it is upon your head—
> Strike a blow as heroes may.

'Furthermore,

> When from assailants to withdraw   (18)
> Useless does the wise man see,
> He goes to battle ready for
> Death beside the enemy.

'Further,

> When fighting, one alive could stay,   (19)
> But not to fight makes ruin sure.
> Then, as all the sages say,
> It is surely time for war.'

Deliberating thus, the crab cut off the crane's neck and killed
him.

"That is why I spoke about the crane eating all the fish,"
the minister remarked. But King Dapple said again, "Minister,

just listen to me. I have thought about this. If Cloudcolour is installed as the king in Karpūra island, he will send us the best of all the things that are to be found there. We can then live in great luxury on the Vindhyā mountain."

"Sire," Farsighted said with a smile,

"One who gives himself to glee,   (20)
With thought of something yet to be—
Ridicule is his certain lot,
Like the priest who broke the pot."

"How did that happen?" asked the king. The minister narrated

The Priest who fantasized

In the town of Devīkota there was a priest named Deva Śarmā. He was presented with an earthenware pot full of barley flour on the sacred occasion when the sun transits the sign of Aries. Troubled by the hot weather, he went with his pot to a potter's shed full of other vessels, and lay down in a corner there. Then, with a stick in his hand to guard the flour, he began to think:

'If I sell this pot of flour, I will get ten cowrie coins. With them I will buy pots and pitchers here itself and, selling them again, increase my money many times over. With that I will buy and sell betel nuts, garments and other articles, and earn a fortune of hundreds of thousands. Then I will marry four wives. I will love the youngest and prettiest one among them most of all, and when the others become jealous and quarrel with her, I will get angry and beat them thus with the stick.'

Speaking to himself in this way, he hurled the stick and smashed his pot of flour. Many other pots also got broken. The potter arrived on hearing the noise, and saw the state of his vessels. He abused the priest roundly, and threw him out of his shed.

~

"That is why I referred to thinking something yet to be,"
said the minister. The king then took the vulture aside and
said, "Please advise me, Father. What should be done?" The
vulture said:

> "When kings or elephants go astray,   (21)
> Filled with pride, with rut inflamed,
> It is those who guide their way
> Who are certain to be blamed.

"Listen, sire. Was the fortress captured by the arrogance of
our army, or by a plan put into effect by Your Majesty's
prowess?"

"It was Your Honour's plan," said the king.

"If my advice is to be taken," the vulture continued,
"then let us go back to our own country. We are on foreign
soil. If war is resumed with an adversary of equal strength,
and the rains set in, even returning home will be difficult
for us. We should make peace, both for the sake of our
welfare as well as our prestige, and go. We have already
won the glory of capturing the fortress. So, this is my advice.
For,

> One who fears not to ignore   (22)
> His master's piques or sympathies
> But, placing duty to the fore,
> Will speak truths that may not please:
> By him alone, it's clear to see,
> A king is aided properly.

"As Bṛhaspati[5] himself did say: (23)

'One should any doubt avoid
That in a war both parties may
Sometimes together get destroyed.'

"Further,

Which person, who is not a fool,   (24)
Will stake himself, his kingly rule,
His allies, arms, and reputation
Upon the dubious oscillation
Of the balance, never sure,
Which is what indeed is war?

"Furthermore,

One should look for peaceful ties   (25)
With even those of equal[6] size,
For victory is never sure
In the grim contest of war.
Were not Sunda and Upasunda
Peers, yet slain by one another?"

"How did that happen?" the king asked. The minister
narrated

The Two Ogres

Once upon a time there were two ogres named Sunda and
Upasunda, who were brothers. They desired sovereignty over
all the three worlds, and for this they prayed for long to
the moon-crested god, subjecting themselves to great physical
torment. The god was at last satisfied, and asked them to
choose a boon.

Meanwhile the two brothers had been possessed by
Sarasvatī, the goddess of speech, who made them ask Śiva
for something quite different from what they had wished to

request. 'Lord, if you are pleased with both of us,' they said, 'then give us your beloved consort, the lady Pārvatī.'

The god was incensed. But since it was imperative that a boon once promised should be granted, he handed Pārvatī over to the two dolts. Both coveted her for her beauty and grace, and lusted for her in their hearts. But sin is darkness, and the two ogres, who could destroy the world, began to quarrel, each saying, 'She is mine.'

At last the two agreed that they should consult a mediator. The same god then appeared in the guise of an old priest and stood before them. 'We have obtained her by our own prowess,' they asked the priest, 'to which of us two does she belong?' The priest replied:

'A priest is reckoned to be blest   (26)
When his wisdom is the best;
A warrior when he has great power;
A merchant, when of wealth a tower;
And a servant blest will be
By service to the other three.

'Now both of you follow the dharma of warriors,' the priest continued, 'so your duty is to fight.'

'He is right!' the two brothers exclaimed on hearing the priest. They were both of equal strength. Striking one another at the same time, they destroyed themselves simultaneously.

~

"That is why I spoke about seeking peace with even those who are of equal power," said the vulture. "Why did not Your Honour say this earlier?" the king asked. "Did Your Majesty listen in full to what I said?" the minister responded. "Even then, it was not on my advice that this war commenced. Goldegg has qualities which fit him to be an ally, not an adversary. As it is said,

These seven one may categorize   (27)
As fit for being made allies:
Those who will be true in trust,
The noble-minded, and the just,
The base, those who their kin unite,
The strong, and those who win a fight.

One who is true will truth protect   (28)
And, once allied, will not defect.
The noble one, it's always seen
Will risk his life but not be mean.

If a just king is attacked   (29)
In war, by all he will be backed;
His people's love, his virtues sweet,
Will make him very hard to beat.

When you must destruction face,   (30)
Make peace even with the base.
For without their sanctuary,
The noble ones face jeopardy.

As bamboo thick with thorny shoot   (31)
In clusters, one cannot uproot,
So it is with those who stand
With their kin, a close-knit band.

Nowhere says the scriptural lore   (32)
That with the mighty one should war.
Never can the rain cloud go
Against the way the wind does blow.

As with Jamadagni's son,[7]   (33)
The fame of him, who's often won

In battle, keeps the multitude
Always everywhere subdued.

He who has many battles won,   (34)
When he makes his peace with one,
His fame will make one's enemies
Also quickly sue for peace.

"This king has many virtues," the vulture concluded. "We
should therefore make peace with him."

~

The goose continued, 'Spy, everything has been understood.
Go now, and come back with more information.'

The king then asked the goose, 'Minister, who are the
people with whom peace should not be made? I would like
to know that also.'

'I will tell you, sire,' the minister replied. 'Listen

The child, the dotard, the invalid,   (35)
One denounced by his own kin,
A coward, one who's full of greed,
And one whose servants share this sin;

One whose aides have no devotion,   (36)
One given up to luxury,
Whose mind is full of vacillation,
Whose words are full of blasphemy;

One who's plain unlucky, or   (37)
One obsessed by destiny,
One with famine at his door,
Or plagued by problems military;

One lacking time appropriate, (38)
One with many enemies,
In exile, or an apostate:
Twenty types of men are these.

With them do not effect a peace, (39)
And let the fighting continue,
For, by war, these categories
You can always fast subdue.

A child knows not the consequence (40)
Of using or not using might,
Nor has it any influence;
So, for it none wish to fight.

The aged and the invalid (41)
Have neither zest nor energy:
Their own men bring down both, indeed
Of this no doubt can ever be.

One whom all his kin disown, (42)
It's easy to put away.
Win them with some favours shown,
And him they themselves will slay.

The coward, running away from war, (43)
Guarantees his own destruction;
And one whose men are insecure
Will, in conflict, face desertion.

The miser does not booty share, (44)
Therefore his men will not fight;
And if they thoughts covetous bear,
They'll also kill him for a mite.

One whose aides are disaffected (45)

Will, in war, abandoned be;
And one to pleasures much addicted,
Can be struck at easily.

Those who in council vacillate, (46)
Their ministers all despise
And ignore in tasks of state,
Because their will is imprecise.

The blasphemer who does revile (47)
Gods and prelates all the while—
By dharma's power, it is known,
He will perish on his own.
And so will he, whose luck is out—
Of this there is not any doubt.

Success or adversity— (48)
Both are due to destiny.
Thinking this is always true,
The fatalist will nothing do.

One by famine overtaken (49)
Will perish on his own, 'tis sure;
And one by troops rebellious shaken
Has no strength to enter war.

In exile one can easily (50)
Be slain by foes insignificant.
A crocodile, though small it be,
In water, drowns the elephant.

Like a dove midst birds of prey (51)
Is one with many enemies.
He perishes soon, whichever way,
Terrified, he tries to flee.

One untimely gone to fight   (52)
Gets killed, as was the crow at night,
By one with opportunity—
The owl who could in darkness see.

Peace one must not ever make   (53)
With him who does true faith forsake.
Apostates, though allies be,
Such always is their perfidy
That there will not be much delay
Before from one they turn away.

'I will also tell you this,' the goose continued. 'There are six means employed in statecraft. They are: making war; making peace or an alliance; mounting an expedition; halting and waiting; taking shelter; and making a feint. There are five subjects to be determined through counsel and consultation. These are: the methods for initiating a measure; the maximum mobilization of men and money; the management of time and space; insuring against accidents; and the successful conclusion of an enterprise. Expedients of policy there are four: conciliation, inducement, disruption and force. And there are three sources of state power: the leader's own energy and charisma; the quality of advice he gets; and the resources at his disposal. Those who wish for victory should always pay attention to all of these. Thus they can achieve greatness.

Hard to gain is Sovereignty—   (54)
She cannot even for the fee
Of giving up one's life be bought.
But though capricious, this cocotte
Will running to the mansions go
Of those who well all policy know.

'And as it is said,

One who keeps his treasury   (55)
Portioned well and equally,
Whose spies covertly ply their trade,
Whose counsels are in secret made,
Who never speaks unpleasantly:
He'll rule the earth right to the sea.

'But, sire, although his great minister, the vulture, has
proposed that peace be made, this has not been accepted
so far by the king because of his arrogance at their recent
victory. In this situation we should do the following. Our
friend, the stork named Mahābala or Greatmight, is the king
of the isle of Simhala. Let him create a disturbance in Jambu
island. For,

The brave man, with a compact force   (56)
To secret movements takes recourse,
And harasses the enemy
Till he is troubled equally.
When both suffer adversities
They will, for certain, look for peace.'

The king agreed and despatched a crane named Vichitra or
Speckled to Simhala island with a confidential letter.

Meanwhile the spy returned and informed the king, 'Sire,
listen to what happened there. The vulture told his king that
as Cloudcolour had stayed here for a long time, he would
know if King Goldegg did or did not have the qualities
appropriate for an ally.

King Dapple then summoned Cloudcolour, and asked,
'Crow, what is Goldegg like? Also, how is his minister, the
goose?'

'Sire,' said the crow, 'King Goldegg is as noble a soul
as Yudhiṣṭhira.[8] As for the goose, a minister like him will
not be found anywhere.'

'If that is so,' the king responded, 'then how did he get

taken in by you?' Cloudcolour smiled and said, 'Sire,

> Does cheating need ingenuity (57)
> With those who trust in you do place?
> Can murder ever manly be
> Of one who sleeps in your embrace?

'Listen, sire, the minister knew what I was as soon as he saw me. But the king was a noble soul, and therefore I was able to deceive him. As it is said,

> One who thinks a knave to be (58)
> Like himself in honesty
> Is deceived, as was the priest
> By rogues who robbed him of his beast.'

'How did that happen?' the king asked. Cloudcolour narrated

The Priest and the Three Rogues

'There was a priest who arranged a fire sacrifice in Gautama's forest. He went to another village to buy a goat for the sacrifice and, as he was returning with the animal on his shoulder, he was observed by three rogues. "If we can get hold of this goat by some stratagem," the rogues said to themselves, "it will indeed be a proof of our wit and wiles." They then took position under three separate trees at intervals of a *krosa*[9] each on the path taken by the priest, and lay in wait.

As the priest passed by, the first rogue called out, "O priest, why are you carrying a dog on your shoulder?" "It is not a dog," replied the priest, "it is a goat for the sacrifice." But when the second rogue standing further down the road said the same thing, the priest put the goat down on the ground and inspected it repeatedly. Finally he put it back on his shoulder and went on, but his mind wavered with doubt. For,

> Even good men's minds, it's true,   (59)
> Waver when the wicked speak;
> And trusting them, they perish too,
> Like Spotted Ear, the camel meek.'

'How did that happen?' the king asked. The crow narrated

The Credulous Camel

*I*n a certain forest region there lived a lion named Madotkaṭa or Choleric. His three servants, a crow, a tiger and a jackal, were once wandering about when they saw a camel who had got separated from his herd. 'From where have you come, sir?' they asked him, and he told them his story. They then took him and presented him before the lion who granted him asylum and safe conduct, and named him Ćitrakarṇa or Spotted Ear.

Once it rained heavily. The lion fell ill and could not hunt, and the servants had nothing to eat. Filled with anxiety, they told each other, 'Let us so arrange things that the master at least kills Spotted Ear. What have we got to do with this eater of thorns?' 'But how will this be possible?' the tiger asked. 'The master has already favoured him with a safe conduct.'

'At this moment the master is so famished,' the jackal observed, 'that he will even commit a heinous sin. For,

> A woman will her child forsake   (60)
> When hunger's pangs she can't evade,
> As will the famished mother snake
> Eat eggs that she herself has laid:
> What sins will not the starving do?
> Men grown gaunt turn pitiless too.

'Further,

> One who's hungry, one dead drunk, (61)
> Or gone mad, or in a funk,
> Or filled with anger, or with greed,
> Or careless in both thought and deed,
> Or in a hurry, or simply tired,
> Or by carnal passion fired:
> One who is in such a state,
> He cannot virtue appreciate.'

After having deliberated in this way, they all went to the lion. 'Have you got something to eat?' the lion asked. 'Nothing at all,' they said, 'despite every effort.'

'How then will we survive?' the lion remonstrated. 'Sire,' said the crow, 'the food is there at our disposal. It is because we reject it that we are facing disaster.'

'And what food is at our disposal here?' the lion asked. 'Spotted Ear,' the crow whispered in his ear.

The lion touched the ground and then both his ears in horror. 'I have kept him there after promising him safe conduct,' he said. 'How is this possible? Besides,

> Not gift of land, or cows, or gold, (62)
> Nor that of foodgrains can it be—
> Of all the gifts, we have been told,
> The greatest is security.

'Further,

> The sacred sacrificial fires (63)
> It's known, can fulfill all desires.
> But the fruit that they ordain
> Is the same that one may gain
> By protecting faithfully
> Those who come for sanctuary.'

'It is not for the master to kill him,' said the crow. 'It is for us to so arrange matters that he will himself agree to donate his own person.' On hearing this the lion kept silent.

The crow then hatched a conspiracy. On getting an opportunity, he took all the others and went to the lion. 'Sire, we have not found any food despite every effort,' he said. 'The master is fatigued with so much fasting. So, let him eat my flesh now. For,

The master is indeed the root   (64)
Which does all the subjects bear.
Man's endeavours will give fruit
Both tree and root when they do rear.'

'My good fellow!' the lion exclaimed, 'it will be better for me to give up life than even think of such a possibility.'

The same offer was made by the jackal which also the lion declined. 'May the master live on my flesh,' the tiger then said, and the lion replied, 'This can never be proper.'

Convinced by all this, Spotted Ear also offered himself similarly. Even as he was speaking, the tiger ripped his belly open. Thus was he slain and devoured by the rest.

'That is why I spoke about the wavering of even good minds,' the crow concluded. 'After listening to the third rogue, the priest was convinced that his own mind had got confused. So, he discarded the goat, had a purificatory bath, and went home, while the rogues took away the beast and ate it up. That is why I referred to the person who judges a knave as himself.'

'Cloudcolour, how did you manage to stay so long among our enemies, and keep them pleased?' the king asked. 'What cannot be done, sire,' replied Cloudcolour, 'by one who

wants to do his master's work, or acts in his own interest?
Look,

> Do not men bear on their brow   (65)
> the wood they will in fire throw,
> And rivers wash the feet of trees
> Even as they destroy these?

'And it is said, similarly,

> To get a thing for which they care   (66)
> The wise will even enemies bear
> On their backs, as did the snake
> Who hunted frogs, a meal to make.'

'How did that happen?' the king asked. Cloudcolour narrated

The Cunning Old Snake

*I*n a ruined garden there was an aged snake named
Mandaviṣa or Dullvenom, who had become so old that he
was unable even to search for food. So he just kept lying
by the side of a pond. There he was seen by a frog, who
asked, 'Why is it that you are not searching for food?'

'Let me be, good sir,' said the serpent, 'What is the point
of putting such questions to someone as ill-starred as myself?'

This aroused the frog's curiosity. 'Tell me, nevertheless,'
he insisted. Finally the snake said, 'Good sir, in Brahmapura
there lives the learned priest Kauṇḍinya. He had a son,
about twenty years of age, who was endowed with every
good quality. Unfortunately, I was wicked enough to bite
this boy, who was named Suśila.

'Seeing his son dead, Kauṇḍinya swooned with grief and
fell rolling on the ground. All his kinsmen and other
inhabitants of Brahmapura gathered there and sat around
him. As it is said:

Know him to be the comrade true,[10]   (67)
In glee or gloom who stands by you,
In times of famine, anarchy,
In law court and the cemetery.

'Among those present was a person named Kapila who had
just graduated to the status of a householder after completing
his religious studies. He said, "O Kaundinya, you are a fool
to lament like this. Listen,

When one is born, the first embrace   (68)
Is from the midwife, Transience.
The mother takes a later place:
Mourning therefore makes no sense.

Where did all the mighty go   (69)
With cavalcades of splendour rare?
Witness to their passing show
Even now this earth does bear.

"Furthermore,

Ailments in this body bide,   (70)
Misfortunes in wealth reside,
Parting is inbuilt in meeting,
All creation is so fleeting.

This body, we do not see,   (71)
Wastes away continuously.
We notice only when it dies,
Like a vessel liquefies
When it's made of unbaked clay
And filled with water cannot stay.

Death comes closer, day by day,   (72)
To every creature, it is clear,

As step by step, to one on way
To execution, it draws near.

Beauty, youth, of wealth a store, (73)
Power, loved ones we adore,
And life itself are transitory:
For the wise, of this, no doubt can be.

Drifting on the sea's expanse, (74)
As two logs will meet by chance,
And having met, will part perforce—
Such is creatures' intercourse.

As travellers, in some wayside shade, (75)
Rest awhile in journey's course,
Then move on in cavalcade—
Such is creatures' intercourse.

"Further,

Five elements do this frame compose. (76)
What's the need for mourning when
Each one to its own source goes,
And in it is absorbed again?

As many times a person makes (77)
Ties in which he pleasure takes,
So often is some sorrow's dart
Buried deep inside his heart.

One can never hope to be (78)
With anything eternally,
Not even with one's body here,
Not to speak of others dear.

"Besides,

Union surely makes it clear (79)
That parting too will come to be,
As birth the coming does declare
Of death, an inevitability.

Being close to those we love (80)
At the start does pleasant prove,
But as with food from tainted grain,
The end result is full of pain.

"Furthermore,

Just as river currents flow (81)
On, and never backwards go,
Similarly do night and day
Move onwards, taking lives away.

Even good men's company, (82)
On which the world's best joys depend,
Must rank a leading misery,
Because in parting it must end.

Therefore, good men's company, (83)
By the sage is never sought.
To part from them will always be
A sword, the wound from which cannot
But always rankle in the mind:
A balm for it one will not find.

Sāgara[11] and the kings of yore (84)
Did many deeds of merit great,
Yet their good works are no more—
Them also time did obliterate.

As death's sharp sting they think about, (85)
All the strivings of the wise

Go limp, like straps of leather stout
Left soaking under rainy skies.

From that very night, O King,   (86)
When in the womb one comes to stay,
A ceaseless journey will him bring
Nearer death each passing day.

"For those who have thought about the world's transitoriness,
therefore, this grief is merely a display of ignorance. Look,

If separation really was   (87)
Of sorrow the primal cause,
Rather than one's ignorance,
Why should grief's circumference
Then not increase each passing day,
Instead of tending to decay?

"So, look into yourself, good sire, and give up this
lamentation. For,

For crushing blows of bitter grief,   (88)
Sudden too, and fresh withal,
The greatest balm that brings relief
Is not to think of them at all."

'Kaundinya seemed to come to his senses on hearing these
words. "My home is now a hell," he said, getting up. "I
will not live here any more. I will go away, even to the
forest." Kapila spoke again:

"In forests too do problems chase   (89)
Those who follow passion's ways;
And those who can control their senses,
At home itself can do penances.
For home too is a hermitage

For one who subdues passion's rage,
And such works does carry out
As no one can despise or doubt.

"For,

Though misery may your being mar,   (90)
In whatever state of life you are,
Act virtuously with piety,
And everyone treat equally.
The source of virtue does not lie
In emblems which we sanctify.

"And it has been said,

Such people surmount all obstruction   (91)
Who eat but just to life sustain,
And limit sex to procreation,
And only speak to truth maintain.

"Similarly,

The soul is a river deemed to be,   (92)
Self-restraint its holy ford,
Its water, plain veracity,
Its banks, the temper well secured,
Compassion its current true.
O son of Pāndu,[12] to it hie—
Common waters will not do
The inner self to purify.

"And specially,

The world is no more than a stage   (93)
Playing out the agony
Of birth and death, disease and age:

Give it up and happy be.

"For,

> Only pain, it's clear to see,   (94)
> Is actual, not felicity;
> The last is but a term ordained
> For soothing one who's greatly pained."

"This is so," said Kaundinya. Then that grief-stricken priest
cursed me to become a porter of frogs from that very day,'
the snake continued. 'Kapila told him, "Sir, you cannot bear
to take advice even now. Your heart is still full of sorrow.
Nevertheless listen to what you should do,

> With all your strength you should forsake   (95)
> Your ties; if they are hard to break,
> Then keep them only with the pure:
> For this will be a remedy sure.

"Further,

> With all your strength you should eschew   (96)
> Desire; if that's hard to do,
> Then have it just for being free
> Of passion: that's its remedy."

'The fire of Kaundinya's grief was extinguished by the nectar
of Kapila's advice. After listening to it, he formally assumed
the renunciant's staff. As for myself, because of the priest's
curse I stay here to carry frogs.'

The frog then went to his king, who was Jālapāda or
Webfoot, and narrated the snake's story to him. The frog
king came to the garden and climbed upon the back of the
snake who then carried him around, executing a series of
elegant movements.

On the following day the king of the frogs found the snake unable to move. 'Sir, why are you so slow today?' he asked. 'Sire,' replied the serpent, 'I have become weak as I have nothing to eat.'

'We give you leave to eat frogs,' said the frog king. 'I accept this great favour,' the snake replied, and he began to eat the frogs one by one. In due course, when he observed that there were no more left in the pond, he also devoured the frog king.

~

'That is why I spoke about carrying even one's enemies along,' said the crow. 'But leave aside old stories, sire. In my opinion we should make peace with King Goldegg who is entirely suited to be an ally.'

'How can you even think of this, sir?' cried King Dapple. 'He has been defeated by us. If he stays as our vassal, let him do so. If not, we must go to war again.'

Meanwhile the parrot had returned from Jambu island. 'Sire,' he said to Dapple, 'the stork who is the king of Simhala has now attacked and invaded Jambu.'

'What!' exclaimed the king in some confusion. But the vulture said to himself, 'Well done, O goose! Well done, Minister Knowall!'

The king was furious. 'Let the invader watch out,' he cried. 'I will go and extirpate him, root and branch.' Farsighted smiled and said,

'One should not thunder just in vain   (97)
Like autumn clouds which have no rain.
The wise to strangers don't declare
What they can or cannot bear.

'Furthermore,

The king should not simultaneously   (98)
Go to war on many fronts.
An arrogant snake is bound to be
Killed if insect hosts he hunts.

'Why go from here without making peace, sire? Otherwise there will surely be an insurrection after we leave. Furthermore,

One who does not ascertain   (99)
The nature of reality,
But succumbs to anger's strain,
Will extremely sorry be—
As happened to the foolish priest
With his little mongoose beast.'

'How did that happen?' the king asked. Farsighted narrated

The Hasty Priest and the Loyal Mongoose

In the city of Ujjayinī there was a priest named Mādhava whose wife had just had a baby. She asked him to guard the infant and herself went to have a bath. Meanwhile a summons arrived from the king for the priest to receive a gift in the ceremony commemorating the ancestors. The priest was poor, and on getting this news he naturally thought, 'If I do not go immediately, then someone else will get the gift. For,

A gift to give, a gift to take,   (100)
And other work one ought to do,
If one won't quickly undertake,
Time then saps its essence true.

'But there is no one here to guard this child. What should I do?' the priest thought further. 'Well, here is a way. I

have kept this mongoose as a pet for a long time, and
treated it like my own son. I will leave it to guard the child,
and go.'

Having made this arrangement, the priest went away. A
black serpent then approached the child. The mongoose saw
this, and killed the snake, tearing it apart.

When the priest returned, the mongoose came up to him
immediately and rolled with pleasure at his feet. But its
mouth and paws were stained with blood and, seeing it in
this condition, the priest concluded that it had attacked the
child. So he promptly killed the mongoose.

On running inside, when the priest looked about him,
he saw the child lying safe, and a snake lying dead. He
turned then to the mongoose who had served him so well.
His heart filled with emotion, and he was stricken by a deep
sorrow.

~

'That is why I spoke about ascertaining the nature of reality,'
said the vulture. 'Furthermore,

> Anger, lust, and dark delusion,   (101)
> Arrogance and pride and greed—
> All these six deserve exclusion:
> Who gives them up has joy indeed.'

'Is what you have said your final opinion, minister?' asked
the king. 'It is indeed,' the minster replied, 'For,

> A firm and a perceptive mind,   (102)
> To basic interests never blind,
> Taking well-informed decisions,
> Secrecy in consultations—
> In ministers, all of these

Are the supreme qualities.

'And similarly,

> Do not act impetuously. (103)
> Heedlessness is known to be
> In every case the chiefest source
> Of a catastrophic course;
> While success does itself select
> To come to him who will reflect
> Before he starts upon an action:
> For fortune that's his great attraction.

'Therefore, sire, if you are to act on my advice, you should now make peace, and then depart. For,

> Even though sages ordain (104)
> Four methods[13] for your ends to gain,
> That is mere enumeration:
> True success comes from conciliation.'

'How can this be possible?' the king asked. 'Sire, it can be achieved immediately,' said the minister. 'For,

> To please one who does nothing know (105)
> Is easy; and it's easier so
> To please one who has wisdom great.
> But even God cannot placate
> The man whose head has somewhat turned
> With the little he has learned.

'In the present case, specially, this king knows the path of righteousness, and his minister knows everything. I realized this earlier from what their actions demonstrated, as well as from what Cloudcolour said. For,

Virtues which one cannot see, (106)
From actions they can inferred be.
When actions too one does not know,
Their outcomes on them light will throw.

'We have discussed this sufficiently,' the king then said,
'please proceed as you have proposed.' Thus advised, Chief
Minister Vulture went inside the fort, saying, 'Whatever is
needed will be done.'

Meanwhile the crane, who had been sent out as a spy,
came to King Goldegg and told him, 'Sire, Chief Minister
Vulture is coming here to make peace.'

'Minister,' observed the swan king, 'another person with
some ulterior motive is now coming here.' Knowall smiled
and said, 'There is no need for suspicion. Farsighted is a
noble soul. It is only the dull-witted who either do not
suspect anything at all or, conversely, are suspicious of
everything without exception. Just as,

The swan could not see well at night (107)
And, deluded momentarily,
Mistook the stars' reflected light
In the lake for stems of lily.
Even in the morning then,
At the lotus blossoms fair
It chooses not to peck again,
As if shining stars they were.
Folk who have been taken in,
Will even in truth see some sin.

Minds which villains once deceive (108)
Will even the godly not believe.
By hot milk scalded, the schoolboy blows
On even what are curds he knows.

'On our part, sire, we should assemble the best that we can

of jewels and other gifts to receive the vulture with.'

After this had been arranged, the goose received Minister Vulture at the fortress gate, and brought him in with all courtesy to meet the king. The visitor was offered a seat which he assumed.

'All this is yours,' said the goose, 'enjoy this kingdom as you wish.' 'That is so,' added Goldegg.

'It is indeed so,' said Farsighted. 'But at this moment there is no need to speak at length. For,

> With wealth one may the greedy lure,   (109)
> And the stern with acts placatory;
> With fools one lets their fancies soar,
> But the wise must have veracity.

'Further,

> Friends are won by feelings true,   (110)
> Relatives by respect due,
> Spouse and servants may be won
> By gifts, and honours to them done,
> And all the other folk there be,
> One should win by courtesy.

'Therefore you should now make peace with the mighty King Dapple, and let him depart.'

'How is this peace to be effected?' asked the goose. 'Be kind enough to explain that also.' Goldegg added, 'How many kinds of peace can there be?'

'I will explain,' said the vulture. 'Listen,

> Invaded by a stronger force,   (111)
> In stress, and with no other recourse,
> To sue for peace a king should strain,
> In order for more time to gain.

Kapāla, Upahāra, Santāna, Sangata, Upanyāsa, (112-113)
Pratikāra, Samyoga, Puruṣāntara, Adriṣṭanara,
Ādiṣhta, Ātmādiṣhta, Upagraha, Parikraya,
Uċhana, Parabhūṣaṇa, and Skandhopaneya.

These have always lauded been (114)
As treaties of peace sixteen.
This is what the experts state
When they on peace elaborate.

The Kapāla peace is known to be (115)
Strictly based on parity.
The Upahāra has it specified
That one side must a gift provide.

A daughter must one party cede, (116)
Before the Santāna is decreed.
The Sangata, all sages confirm,
Is based upon a friendship firm.

The Sangata equal terms provides (117-118)
For the aims of both the sides.
It alone, one may be sure,
Will throughout their lives endure.
In thick or thin it will not break,
Nor for other reasons' sake.
This is the peace, whose excellence
Is like gold in every sense,
So that peace arrangers all
As "The Golden" do it call.

The peace arrangement which intends (119)
The gaining only of one's ends
Is Upanyāsa, said so to be
By those who know diplomacy.

"I did help him in the past, (120)
He will reciprocate at last":
A peace made on this consideration—
Pratikāra is its appellation.

"I will help him, so will he (121)
Reciprocate due help to me":
This is Pratikāra too,
As Rāma with Sugrīva[14] did do.

A peace agreement which is signed (122)
With a single purpose well-defined,
Its terms secured with calculation—
Samyoga is its appellation.

When agreement is assured (123)
That each side's interests be secured
By leading warriors of its own,
That peace is Puruṣāntara known.

When it is the foe's condition (124)
That his interest have protection
By the other side alone,
That is Adṛṣṭapuruṣha known.

When a powerful enemy (125)
Claims portion of your territory
As for peace a precondition,
That then has the appellation
Ādiṣṭa from those who know
How such peace agreements go.

A peace by one's own army made (126)
As Ātmadiṣṭa, experts grade.
To save your life, when you concede
Everything, is Upagraha decreed.

To save remaining property (127)
By ceding part of treasury,
Or half of it, or even all:
Parikraya, experts do it call.

The peace Ucchanna comes to be (128)
By ceding rich territory.
The gift of only its produce
Is called the Parabhūṣaṇa truce.

Where a specific lot is gifted— (129)
As much as on the back is lifted—
That the arbitrators all
The Skandhopaneya peace do call.

It should be known that real peace (130)
Comes only in four categories:
Friendship, mutual obligations,
Gifts, and marital relations.

In my view there is but one (131)
Peace: it is through presents won.
All the other types will be
Lacking in true amity.

A stronger enemy force will not (132)
Withdraw till it has something got.
Apart from gifts, it's clear to see,
A way to peace there cannot be.'

'Listen to me, first,' said the goose.

"This is mine, and this is not"— (133)
Thus do the small-minded see.
The large-hearted have always thought
The world itself a family.[15]

'Furthermore,

> As dirt to see the wealth of others; (134)
> And wives of other men as mothers;
> In creatures all, yourself reflected—
> Who sees thus is the man perfected.[16]

'Your Honour is great-hearted as well as wise,' said the swan king. 'Please advise me what I should do now.'

'Ah, why do you speak like this,' said Farsighted the vulture,

> 'The mind will fail, the body break, (135)
> This frame will perish any day.
> Who indeed will for its sake,
> Go counter to the righteous way?

> 'Fleeting, as the moon's reflection (136)
> In water, is all life's confection.
> This being well understood,
> One must always do what's good.

> Perceiving this world to be (137)
> Like a mirage, transitory,
> With the good keep company
> For virtue and for felicity.

'So let that indeed be done. That is my opinion. For,

> A thousand times one may recourse (138)
> To sacrifices of the horse,
> But in a balance this compare
> With the worth that truth does bear.
> And truth is always found to be
> Greater than such ceremony.

'Therefore, let there be made between these two kings the golden peace, of which truth is the touchstone.'

'I agree,' said Knowall. Minister Farsighted was thereafter honoured by King Goldegg with gifts of ornaments and garments. Greatly pleased, he took the goose to meet the peacock king. On the vulture's advice, King Dapple spoke to Knowall with great respect and generosity, and sent him back to Goldegg after accepting the peace which had been proposed.

'Sire,' said Farsighted, 'our purpose has been accomplished. Let us now go back and return to our own home in the Vindhyā mountain.' Thereafter they all returned to their own land and obtained whatever their hearts desired.

~

'*T*ell me,' said Viṣṇu Śarma, 'what more shall I relate to you?'

'By your grace we have come to understand affairs of state in all their aspects,' the princes replied. 'We are very happy indeed.'

'If that is so,' said Viṣṇu Śarma, 'then may this too come to be:

May peace and joy forever be (139)
With all the kings in victory.
May good men be free of woe
And glory of the virtuous grow.
May ministers always bear
On their breasts that mistress fair,
Good policy, to constantly
Kiss the face; and may there be
Every day, for one and all
A great and happy festival.

'And this too,

As long as dwells the lord with lunar crest,   (140)
Within the mountain maiden's warm embrace;[17]
As long as Lakshmī gleams on Viṣṇu's breast,
Like lightning's flash in monsoon clouds apace;
As long as shines great Merū's golden peak,
A flame whose very sparks are like the sun;
So long may this concourse of stories speak
To men. It was by Nārāyaṇa done.

'Furthermore,

To Dhavala Ćandra, Victory!   (141)
An illustrious prince is he,
Through his efforts, this collection
Was writ and put in circulation.'

Notes

Introduction

1. A. L. Basham, *The Wonder that was India*, New York, 1954

2. L. Sternbach, *The Kāvya-Portions in the Kathā-Literature*, vol. II, Meharchand Lachhman Das, Delhi, 1974. This, and the same scholar's *The Hitopadeśa and its Sources*, American Oriental Society 44, New Haven, 1960, contain the two most detailed studies of the *Hitopadeśa* so far.

3. L. Sternbach, *The Kāvya-Portions in the Kathā-Literature*, Vol II.

4. L. Sternbach, *The Hitopadeśa and its Sources*.

5. *The Heetopades of Veeshnoo-Śarma, in a series of connected Fables interspersed with Moral, Prudential & Political Maxims, translated from an ancient manuscript in the Sanskreet Language with Explanatory Notes by Charles Wilkins, Bath: Printed by R. Cruttwell, MDCCLXXXVII.*

6. L. Sternbach, *The Kāvya-Portions in the Kathā-Literature*.

7. *Hitopadeśa of Nārāyaṇa*, ed. P. Peterson, Bombay, 1887.

8. L. Sternbach, *The Kāvya-Portions in the Kathā-Literature*; also A. B. Keith, *A History of Sanskrit Literature*, Oxford, 1920.

9. L. Sternbach, *The Kāvya-portions in the Kathā-Literature*.

10. Ibid.

11. L. Sternbach, *The Hitopadeśa and its Sources*.

12. L. Sternbach, *The Kāvya-Portions in the Kathā-Literature*.

13. L. Sternbach, *The Hitopadeśa and its Sources*.

14. The sourcing of I.16, I.122 and IV.92 is based on *Hitopadeśa of Nārāyaṇa*, ed. M. R. Kale, Bombay, 1896, reprinted, Delhi, 1989.

15. A. L. Basham, *The Wonder that was India*, New York, 1954.

16. *Subhāshita Samgraha*, vol. I, compiled by K.A.S. Iyer, Sahitya Akademi New Delhi, 1971

17. D.H.H. Ingalls (tr.), *Sanskrit Poetry*, Harvard University Press, Cambridge, 1965.

18. L. Sternbach, *The Hitopadeśa and its Sources*.

19. *Hitopadeśa of Nārāyaṇa*, ed. M. R. Kale, Bombay, 1896, reprinted, Delhi 1989.

Book I. *Mitralābha* / Gaining Friends

1. So called because the lilies which bloomed at night were believed to do so under the moon's influence.

2. Because the elephant is seen to squirt dust over itself no sooner than it is washed.

3. The cobra was believed to have a precious gem inside its hood.

4. The mythical king of the serpents had a thousand heads.

The snake's forked tongue is also described as twinned.

5. A religious observance, in which young virgins are reverenced as living embodiments of the goddess during the festival of Navarātrī, is still prevalent in parts of India and Nepal.

Book II. *Suhrdbheda* / Splitting Partners

1. The sage Bṛhaspati, a symbol of wisdom, is the preceptor of the gods. Also mentioned in the Prologue after verse 42.

2. In an episode in the epic *Mahābhārata*, the divine incarnation Krishna was bitterly abused and cursed by Śiśupāla, the king of Ćedi. Krishna long ignored the diatribe, but eventually he killed the king when the latter's vituperation crossed a certain limit. The implication here is that noble people prefer to ignore discourteous behaviour by the base.

3. A small coin, in its time equivalent to one-sixty-fourth of rupee.

4. Śakuni was the uncle and evil genius of the Kaurava king Duryodhana who was defeated in the great war of the *Mahābhārata*. Śakaṭāra was the minister of King Nanda who was overthrown by Ćandragupta Maurya.

5. The *gandharva* rite was one of the eight forms of marriage recognized by ancient law. It dispensed with parental consent and other rituals.

6. This and verse II.64 have one identical line in the original.

7. The three sources of state power postulated by ancient Indian political theorists are described in Book IV, in the prose portion between verses 53 and 54.

8. It was believed that this animal always died while giving birth.

9. These are *dharma* (virtue), *artha* (profit) and *kāma* (pleasure). The fourth human goal, *moksha* (salvation), is spiritual and not worldly. See also Prologue, verse 26.

Book III. *Vigraha* / War

1. Markings on the surface of the moon constitute a rabbit in Indian folklore.

2. The reference is to a person from the Brahmin or priestly caste.

3. In to order to protect the world the god Śiva swallowed the cosmic poison which he alone could endure. However the poison was so strong that it turned the god's throat blue. The verse refers to this myth, but is also a dig at the Brahmin caste. See also verse II.95.

4. The thought being conveyed is that cool heads can surmount great difficulties.

5. According to tradition, Ćānakya brought about the overthrow of King Nanda of Magadha, and the succession of Ćandragupta Maurya, a contemporary of Alexander the Great. Considered a master of diplomacy, Ćānakya's feats are described in the sixth-century play *Mudrārākshasa* by Viśākha Datta. The political treatise *Arthaśāstra* and various verses are ascribed to Ćānakya as noted in the Introduction. See also note II.4 above.

6. The trunk, the head, two tusks and four legs.

7. A salutation expressing the most profound reverence, the *Sāṣṭānga* is so called as it is performed with eight parts of the body—the two feet, knees and hands, the chest

and the forehead—touching the ground. The term also occurs in Book II.

8. Semi-divine beings. Their chief is Kubera, the god of wealth.

Book IV. *Sandhi* / Peace

1. In the original text this verse is the same as I.119.

2. Same as II.117.

3. Same as Prologue, verse 29.

4. This and the next two verses are almost the same as I.57, II.169 and II.168 respectively in the original text, except for slight differences.

5. See note II.1.

6. i.e. not to speak of those who are more powerful.

7. The warrior sage Paraśurāma, a divine incarnation, who defeated all the kings of his time.

8. A hero of the epic *Mahābhārata* who was famous for his virtue as well as lack of guile.

9. A unit of distance, about three kilometres.

10. The same as I.74.

11. A mythical king from whose name is derived a Sanskrit word for the sea.

12. The verse, addressed to a character in the *Mahābhārata*, occurs in the epic's Udyoga Parvan section, (39/40.21).

13. *Sāma*, *dāma*, *bhéda* and *danḍa* are the four expedients of policy already enumerated in prose between IV.53 and IV.54, and also mentioned in III.40. The first, denoting conciliation, is the most preferable method. The last, denoting force, is the least preferable.

14. A reference to the epic *Rāmāyaṇa*. Rāma agreed to help Sugrīva regain the throne, and Sugrīva in turn agreed to help Rāma search for his abducted wife.

15. Same as I.71.

16. Same as I.14.

17. The reference is to the god Śiva and his consort, the goddess Pārvati. He is described often as one who bears the crescent moon on his forehead, (cf. Prologue, verse 1). She is the daughter of the Himālaya mountain. The next line refers to the other main divine couple of the Hindu pantheon.